THE INNER GAME
OF TENNIS

W. Timothy Gallwey has produced a series of bestselling Inner Game books, which set forth a new methodology for the development of personal and professional excellence in a variety of fields. He got his start as a nationally ranked tennis player and later captained the Harvard University tennis team. While on sabbatical from his career in college administration, Gallwey worked as a tennis instructor in Monterey, California. He soon discovered that traditional teaching wasn't as effective as simply inviting his students to focus on awareness. Players using Gallwey's methods improved far more rapidly than usual, without the burden of self-criticism or trying so hard to 'do it right'. By quieting self-interference, they were more able to tap into their natural abilities with greater ease.

From this discovery came Gallwey's first book, *The Inner Game of Tennis*, which has sold over two million copies. Other books in the Inner Game series include applications to golf, music, work and stress. For the last twenty years Gallwey has been introducing the Inner Game approach to corporations looking for better ways to manage change. In the years after his first book's release, readers even began to employ the Inner Game methods to their lives off court, and Tim moved into applying the Inner Game methods of change to corporate work. His long-term clients included Apple, AT&T, the Coca Cola Company, and Rolls Royce. Gallwey's work has often been credited as the foundation of the new fields of corporate and life coaching. Tim's newest focus lies in using modern communication technology and online tools to make his methodology available globally. He lives in Malibu, California.

THE INNER GAME OF TENNIS

The Ultimate Guide to the
Mental Side of Peak Performance

W. TIMOTHY GALLWEY

PAN BOOKS

First published 1975 by Jonathan Cape Ltd

First published in the UK 1986 by Pan Books

This edition published 2015 by Pan Books
an imprint of Pan Macmillan
The Smithson, 6 Briset Street, London EC1M 5NR
Associated companies throughout the world
www.panmacmillan.com

ISBN 978-1-4472-8850-3

Copyright © W. Timothy Gallwey, 1974
Foreword Copyright © Geoff Beattie, 2015

The right of W. Timothy Gallwey to be identified as the
author of this work has been asserted by him in accordance
with the Copyright, Designs and Patents Act 1988.

The extract from 'The Hollow Men' by T. S. Eliot on p. 53
is reproduced by kind permission of Faber & Faber Ltd

Pan Macmillan does not have any control over, or any responsibility for,
any author or third party websites referred to in or on this book.

15

A CIP catalogue record for this book is available from the British Library.

Printed and bound by CPI Group (UK) Ltd, Croydon, CR0 4YY

Visit www.panmacmillan.com to read more about all our books
and to buy them. You will also find features, author interviews and
news of any author events, and you can sign up for e-newsletters
so that you're always first to hear about our new releases.

for my mother and father,
who brought me to the Game,
and for Maharaji,
who showed me what Winning is

What is the real game?
It is a game in which the heart is entertained,
the game in which you are entertained.
It is the game you will win.

MAHARAJI

CONTENTS

FOREWORD

Let it Be

TODAY, MOST PEOPLE IN THE WORLD OF SPORT RECOGNIZE THAT success and failure are not decided solely on the pitch, in the ring or on the tennis court. They are just as often decided in the mind, sometimes before the players have even entered the arena. We watch boxers standing toe to toe and we can see fear flit across the eyes and mouth of one of the fighters, and we know that the game is already up. These days commentators will also point out what they have detected, just in case we have missed it, even when that facial expression is fast and fleeting and soon concealed by the mask of a half-smile. Experienced commentators understand that we, the viewer, are interested these days in reading the emotional state of the fighters and that we want to understand the psychology of the fight to see how it affects the outcome. The commentators have their own way of drawing our attention to it. 'I don't think that the challenger is up for this tonight, it's a big step for him.' And we nod along in agreement, aware already – perhaps even before the boxer himself – that the fight is over before it has even begun.

We are all believers in the importance of the mind in sport these days, and, to some extent, we are even psychologically literate. We are familiar with the phrases 'choking', 'non-verbal leakage' and 'emotional suppression'; we even know a little about the vocabulary for different sorts of personalities and what drives our favourite players. We know a little about the famous 'chimp paradox', developed by the psychiatrist Steve Peters, which offers a 'fun' take on some very basic neuroscience, but with important endorsements from some very satisfied clients – British Cycling, SkyProCycling, Ronnie O'Sullivan, England Rugby, Liverpool Football Club, the England football squad. We may even have heard former England football captain Steven Gerrard talking about 'controlling his inner chimp', and wondered exactly what he has done to get it back in its box. And all this talk and guided observation has seeped into how we think. We watch the England football team line up to take penalties and we analyse them ourselves from the comfort of our armchair. We shout back at the screen at the manager's choice. 'Not him, please not him. It's all over his face. He's lost his confidence; he doesn't want to take a penalty. Can't you see the expression on his face?'

Sometimes we are even right in our predictions (we are right more often than not when it comes to the England football team and penalties), and this reinforces our belief in our ability as intuitive psychologists and the importance of mind-reading in that great competitive domain of sport. We look at great teams or players and reason that the best coaches and managers may be brilliant tacticians, but first and foremost they are great psychologists. They can read their players, motivate them, and more than that, they can understand them. Not in the everyday sense of 'I understand what you are going through: I can feel your pain', but in the much harder sense of 'I can predict how you are going to play today against that opponent in front of those fans, given what you have been through in the past few weeks.' The great managers and coaches have considerable insight into what makes players tick.

But it was not always like this. There was an era in sport when the inner game was rarely taken seriously. Into that void, in the mid-seventies, came a gem of a book called *The Inner Game of Tennis* by Tim Gallwey. The message was simple: 'neither mastery nor satisfaction can be found in the playing of any game without giving some attention to the relatively neglected skills of the inner game. This is the game that takes place in the mind of the player, and it is played against such obstacles as lapses in concentration, nervousness, self-doubt and self-condemnation. In short, it is played to overcome all habits of mind which inhibit excellence in performance.' Gallwey, a tennis player and coach, and not a psychologist, aimed to teach us to play that inner game better. His thesis emerged from what he had witnessed on the tennis court. The seventies seem a long time ago, and occasionally the language of the book (and one or two of the anecdotes) do seem from a different, and nostalgic, era ('freaking out', for example, is a general term used for an upset mind). This is a world of mini-skirts and new dances ('the Monkey, the Jerk and the Swim') and the imagined giant computers of the future ('larger than three Empire State Buildings') with the capacity of a modern smartphone. But, importantly, the book is premised on a very sound principle that has more than stood the test of time. The simple idea underpinning the book is that human beings do not actually have a single mind (which makes the mind-reading of the modern pundit all the more problematic), they have two. They have a conscious mind and an unconscious mind, with both systems underpinned by different neural circuitry, and the interaction between these two different systems might hold the key not just to success in sport but too much else in life besides.

Gallwey's breakthrough came from observing players on the court in front of him, and listening to what they were saying. What he witnessed was players carrying out endless dialogues with themselves. You can imagine the conversations between 'I' (the conscious self/the person who gives the instructions) and 'myself' (the unconscious, automatic self/the person who performs the action). 'Come on, Tom, meet the ball in front of you.' 'Keep your eyes on the ball.' And then the endless criticism: 'How many more mistakes?' 'Stop doing that.' 'You're useless.'

Gallwey calls the conscious self 'Self 1', and the unconscious, automatic self 'Self 2'. He starts with the assumption that the way Self 1 talks to Self 2 might hold the key to sporting success and failure. He tells us to imagine these two components of the mind as different people and then to imagine what we would think of the relationship between these two individuals if we were to overhear what was being said in the endless, repetitive and often insulting instructions given by Self 1 to his or her silent partner. Gallwey writes: 'It seems as though Self 1 doesn't think Self 2 hears well, or has a short memory, or is stupid. The truth is, of course, that Self 2, which includes the unconscious mind and nervous system, hears everything, never forgets anything, and is anything but stupid. After hitting the ball firmly once, he knows forever which muscles to contract to do it again. That's his nature.' But how do you stop the judgmental Self 1 doing this? How do you set the unconscious, automatic mind free? How do you break bad habits, which are unconsciously executed and often carried out without any conscious reflection at all?

Gallwey dismisses some ideas quickly. The power of positive thinking was making a big splash at the time and has continued to do so in various guises through cognitive behavioural therapy (CBT). So too has the training of optimism by focusing on our everyday habitual thoughts and by substituting positive thoughts for negative ones. Indeed, it has given rise to a whole new branch of contemporary psychology called 'positive psychology' (although it is not without its critics). Gallwey himself is quite critical of this way of doing things. He says 'The substituting of a kind of "positive hypnotism" for a previous habit of "negative hypnotism" may appear at least to have short-range benefits, but I have always found that the honeymoon ends all too soon.' His reason for this rejection is that positive and negative evaluations are always in a symbiotic relationship with each other. Gallwey writes 'It is impossible to judge one event as positive without seeing others events as not positive or as negative.' In other words, once you start trying to praise yourself for positive actions, you raise the spectre of criticism. 'That shot was good . . .' Self 1 may be silent for a while, but Self 2 still knows what it is thinking! And in that silence, it still hears the criticism from that great judgmental and disparaging authority figure in the corner, always out to protect itself, always out to criticize others, particularly one other person (Self 2), the one who cannot escape.

So, what is Gallwey's proposed solution? It is about a different type of learning, what psychologists these days might call 'implicit learning'. It's the way we might learn those great new dances – the Monkey, the Jerk or the Swim, in Gallwey's linguistic frame. It's about watching and thinking less, it's about internalizing the visual image in front of you, it's about experimenting with role playing and trying out different routines to increase the range of your game, it's about play and leaving Self 1 aghast at the goings on in this room of fun. Gallwey says it is 'the art of letting go of Self 1 control and letting Self 2 play the game spontaneously.' I would put it stronger than this. It's about locking Self 1 out of the room and pinning a sign on the door. 'No squares allowed, daddyo.' It's about gaining the experience of peace in a moment when the mind is relatively still, it's about seeing the ball differently and listening to it, it's about being aware of your breathing and what it is to be in the moment.

But *The Inner Game of Tennis* would never have had the impact it had if it was just an instructional manual for better tennis. It offers a philosophy of life, a life to be lived in the moment. If you read this book with the sole idea of becoming a winner at tennis, I suspect that Gallwey himself would be more than a little disappointed by your sense of purpose. Indeed, Gallwey attacks the whole notion of competition inherent in sport. 'If I assume that I am making myself more worthy of respect by winning, then I must believe, consciously or unconsciously, that by defeating someone, I am making him less worthy of respect. I can't go up without pushing someone else down.' Gallwey says that sport is not war, and we need to think about it differently, we have to change our metaphorical frame for how we conceptualize it. For Gallwey it's not about winning or losing the match, it's about 'making the maximum effort during every point because I realize that that is where the true value lies.' Gallwey's broad approach is to be found in the Zen philosophy of 'let it be'. 'Letting go means allowing joy to come into your life instead of contriving to have a good time' and the ultimate 'winner' in the end 'stops caring about the outcome and plays all out.'

You can read this book in one sitting, but the ideas will stay with you for a long time. Gallwey clearly hit upon something, and he was very obviously way ahead of his time. Since the mid-nineties psychologists have been devising new methods to measure the operation of the unconscious, automatic system and have explored the relationship between this and the conscious reflective system in some detail. The two systems operate and think differently. In my book *Our Racist Heart? An Exploration of Unconscious Prejudice in Everyday Life* I explored the implications of these two systems for implicit racism in everyday life, now a major research topic. In his bestseller *Thinking, Fast and Slow*, Nobel laureate Daniel Kahneman explored the operation of the two systems for various types of decision making, including economic decision making. Gallwey's little book was very prescient. We may have all forgotten the Monkey, the Jerk or the Swim, but the divided self is still there in tennis, in sport and in life, and we all still have to deal with it, even former England captains battling against their metaphorical inner chimp.

Professor Geoff Beattie,
Edge Hill University, January 2015

INTRODUCTION

EVERY GAME IS COMPOSED OF TWO PARTS, AN OUTER GAME AND AN inner game. The outer game is played against an external opponent to overcome external obstacles, and to reach an external goal. Mastering this game is the subject of many books offering instructions on how to swing a racket, club or bat, and how to position arms, legs or torso to achieve the best results. But for some reason most of us find these instructions easier to remember than to execute.

It is the thesis of this book that neither mastery nor satisfaction can be found in the playing of any game without giving some attention to the relatively neglected skills of the inner game. This is the game that takes place in the mind of the player, and it is played against such obstacles as lapses in concentration, nervousness, self-doubt and self-condemnation. In short, it is played to overcome all habits of mind which inhibit excellence in performance.

We often wonder why we play so well one day and so poorly the next, or why we clutch during competition, or blow easy shots. And why does it take so long to break a bad habit and learn a new one? Victories in the inner game may provide no additions to the trophy case, but they bring valuable rewards which are more permanent and which can contribute significantly to one's success, off the court as well as on.

The player of the inner game comes to value the art of relaxed concentration above all other skills; he discovers a true basis for self-confidence; and he learns that the secret to winning any game lies in not trying too hard. He aims at the kind of spontaneous performance which occurs only when the mind is calm and seems at one with the body, which finds its own surprising ways to surpass its own limits again and again. Moreover, while overcoming the common hang-ups of competition, the player of the inner game uncovers a will to win which unlocks all his energy and which is never discouraged by losing.

There is a far more natural and effective process for learning and doing almost anything than most of us realize. It is similar to the process we all used, but soon forgot, as we learned to walk and talk. It uses the intuitive capabilities of the mind and both the right and left hemispheres of the brain. This process doesn't have to be learned; we already know it. All that is needed is to *un*learn those habits which interfere with it and then to just *let it happen*.

To uncover and explore the potential within the human body is the quest of the Inner Game; in this book it will be explored through the medium of tennis.

THE INNER GAME
OF TENNIS

ONE

Reflections on the Mental Side of Tennis

THE PROBLEMS WHICH MOST PERPLEX TENNIS PLAYERS ARE NOT those dealing with the proper way to swing a racket. Books and professionals giving this information abound. Nor do most players complain excessively about physical limitations. The most common complaint of sportsmen ringing down the corridors of the ages is, "It's not that I don't know what to do, it's that I don't do what I know!" Other common complaints that come constantly to the attention of the tennis pro:

I play better in practice than during the match.

I know exactly what I'm doing wrong on my forehand, I just can't seem to break the habit.

When I'm really trying hard to do the stroke the way it says to in the book, I flub the shot every time. When I concentrate on one thing I'm supposed to be doing, I forget something else.

Every time I get near match point against a good player, I get so nervous I lose my concentration.

I'm my own worst enemy; I usually beat myself.

Most players of any sport run into these or similar difficulties frequently, but it is not so easy to gain practical insight into how to deal with them. The player is often left with such warmed-over aphorisms as "Well, tennis is a very psychological game, and you have to develop the proper mental attitudes" or "You have to be confident and possess the will to win or else you'll always be a loser." But how can one "be confident" or develop the "proper mental attitudes"? These questions are usually left unanswered.

So there seems to be room for comment on the improvement of the mental processes which translate technical information about how to hit a ball into effective action. How to develop the inner skills, without which high performance is impossible, is the subject of *The Inner Game of Tennis*.

THE TYPICAL TENNIS LESSON

Imagine what goes on inside the head of an eager student taking a lesson from an equally eager new tennis pro. Suppose that the student is a middle-aged businessman bent on improving his position on the club ladder. The pro is standing at the net with a large basket of balls, and being a bit uncertain whether his student is considering him worth the lesson fee, he is carefully evaluating every shot. "That's good, but you're rolling your racket face over a little on your follow-through, Mr. Weil. Now shift your weight onto your front foot as you step into the ball . . . Now you're taking your racket back too late . . . Your backswing should be a little lower than on that last shot . . . That's it, much better." Before long, Mr. Weil's mind is churning with six thoughts about what he should be doing and sixteen thoughts about what he shouldn't be doing. Improvement seems dubious and very complex, but both he and the pro are impressed by the careful analysis of each stroke and the fee is gladly paid upon receipt of the advice to "practice all this, and eventually you'll see a big improvement."

I TOO ADMIT TO OVERTEACHING as a new pro, but one day when I was in a relaxed mood, I began saying less and noticing more. To my surprise, errors that I saw but didn't mention were correcting themselves without the student ever knowing he had made them. How were the changes happening? Though I found this interesting, it was a little hard on my ego, which didn't quite see how it was going to get its due credit for the improvements being made. It was an even greater blow when I realized that sometimes my verbal instructions seemed to *decrease* the probability of the desired correction occurring.

All teaching pros know what I'm talking about. They all have students like one of mine named Dorothy. I would give Dorothy a gentle, low-pressured instruction like, "Why don't you try lifting the follow-through up from your waist to the level of your shoulder? The topspin will keep the ball in the court." Sure enough, Dorothy would try hard to follow my instructions. The muscles would tense around her mouth; her eyebrows would set in a determined frown; the muscles in her forearm would tighten, making fluidity impossible; and the follow-through would end only a few inches higher. At this point, the stock response of the patient pro is, "That's better, Dorothy, but relax, don't try so hard!" The advice is good as far as it goes, but Dorothy does not understand how to "relax" while also trying hard to hit the ball correctly.

Why should Dorothy—or you or I—experience an awkward tightening when performing a desired action which is not physically difficult? What happens inside the head between the time the instruction is given and the swing is complete? The first glimmer of an answer to this key question came to me at a moment of rare insight after a lesson with Dorothy: "Whatever's going on in her head, it's too damn much! She's trying so hard to swing the racket the way I told her that she can't focus on the ball." Then and there, I promised myself I would cut down on the quantity of verbal instructions.

My next lesson that day was with a beginner named Paul who had never held a racket. I was determined to show him how to play using as few instructions as possible; I'd try to keep his mind uncluttered and see if it made a difference. So I started by telling Paul I was trying something new: I was going to skip entirely my usual explanations to beginning players about the proper grip, stroke and footwork for the basic forehand. Instead, I was going to hit ten forehands myself, and I wanted him to watch carefully, *not* thinking about what I was doing, but simply trying to grasp a *visual image* of the forehand. He was to repeat the image in his mind several times and then just let his body imitate. After I had hit ten forehands, Paul imagined himself doing the same. Then, as I put the racket into his hand, sliding it into the correct grip, he said to me, "I noticed that the first thing you did was to move your feet." I replied with a noncommittal grunt and asked him to let his body imitate the forehand as well as it could. He dropped the ball, took a perfect backswing, swung forward, racket level, and with natural fluidity ended the swing at shoulder height, perfect for his first attempt! But wait, his feet; they hadn't moved an inch from the perfect ready position he had assumed before taking his racket back. They were nailed to the court. I pointed to them, and Paul said, "Oh yeah, I forgot about them!" The one element of the stroke Paul had tried to remember was the one thing he didn't do! Everything else had been absorbed and reproduced without a word being uttered or an instruction being given!

I was beginning to learn what all good pros and students of tennis must learn: that images are better than words, showing better than telling, too much instruction worse than none, and that trying often produces negative results. One question perplexed me: What's wrong with trying? What does it mean to try *too* hard?

PLAYING OUT OF YOUR MIND

Reflect on the state of mind of a player who is said to be "hot" or "playing in the zone." Is he thinking about how he should hit each shot? Is he thinking at all? Listen to the phrases commonly used to describe a player at his best: "He's out of his mind"; "He's playing over his head"; "He's unconscious"; "He doesn't know what he's doing." The common factor in each of these descriptions is that some part of the mind is not so active. Athletes in most sports use similar phrases, and the best of them know that their peak performance never comes when they're thinking about it.

Clearly, to play unconsciously does not mean to play without consciousness. That would be quite difficult! In fact, someone playing "out of his mind" is more aware of the ball, the court and, when necessary, his opponent. But he is not aware of giving himself a lot of instructions, thinking about how to hit the ball, how to correct past mistakes or how to repeat what he just did. He is conscious, but not thinking, *not over-trying*. A player in this state knows where he wants the ball to go, but he doesn't have to "try hard" to send it there. It just seems to happen—and often with more accuracy than he could have hoped for. The player seems to be immersed in a flow of action which requires his energy, yet results in greater power and accuracy. The "hot streak" usually continues until he starts thinking about it and tries to maintain it; as soon as he attempts to exercise control, he loses it.

To test this theory is a simple matter, if you don't mind a little underhanded gamesmanship. The next time your opponent is having a hot streak, simply ask him as you switch courts, "Say, George, what are you doing so differently that's making your forehand so good today?" If he takes the bait—and 95 percent will—and begins to think about how he's swinging, telling you how he's really meeting the ball out in front, keeping his wrist firm and following through better, his streak invariably will end. He will lose his timing and fluidity as he tries to repeat what he has just told you he was doing so well.

But can one learn to play "out of his mind" on purpose? How can you be consciously unconscious? It sounds like a contradiction in terms; yet this state can be achieved. Perhaps a better way to describe the player who is "unconscious" is by saying that his mind is so concentrated, so focused, that it is *still*. It becomes one with what the body is doing, and the unconscious or automatic functions are working without interference from thoughts. The concentrated mind has no room for thinking how well the body is doing, much less of the how-to's of the doing. When a player is in this state, there is little to interfere with the full expression of his potential to perform, learn and enjoy.

The ability to approach this state is the goal of the Inner Game. The development of inner skills is required, but it is interesting to note that if, while learning tennis, you begin to learn how to focus your attention and how to trust in yourself, you have learned something far more valuable than how to hit a forceful backhand. The backhand can be used to advantage only on a tennis court, but the skill of mastering the art of effortless concentration is invaluable in whatever you set your mind to.

TWO

The Discovery
of the Two Selves

A MAJOR BREAKTHROUGH IN MY ATTEMPTS TO UNDERSTAND THE art of relaxed concentration came when, while teaching, I again began to notice what was taking place before my eyes. Listen to the way players talk to themselves on the court: "Come on, Tom, meet the ball in front of you."

We're interested in what is happening inside the player's mind. Who is telling whom what? Most players are talking to themselves on the court all the time. "Get up for the ball." "Keep it to his backhand." "Keep your eyes on the ball." "Bend your knees." The commands are endless. For some, it's like hearing a tape recording of the last lesson playing inside their head. Then, after the shot is made, another thought flashes through the mind and might be expressed as follows: "You clumsy ox, your grand-mother could play better!" One day I asked myself an important question—Who was talking to whom? Who was scolding and who being scolded? "I'm talking to myself," say most people. But just who is this "I" and who the "myself"?

Obviously, the "I" and the "myself" are separate entities or there would be no conversation, so one could say that within each player there are two "selves." One, the "I," seems to give instructions; the other, "myself," seems to perform the action. Then "I" returns with an evaluation of the action. For clarity let's call the "teller" Self 1 and the "doer" Self 2.

Now we are ready for the first major postulate of the Inner Game: within each player the kind of relationship that exists between Self 1 and Self 2 is the prime factor in determining one's ability to translate his knowledge of technique into effective action. In other words, the key to better tennis—or better anything—lies in improving the relationship between the conscious teller, Self 1, and the natural capabilities of Self 2.

THE TYPICAL RELATIONSHIP BETWEEN SELF 1 AND SELF 2

Imagine that instead of being parts of the same person, Self 1 (teller) and Self 2 (doer) are two separate persons. How would you characterize their relationship after witnessing the following conversation between them? The player on the court is trying to make a stroke improvement. "Okay, dammit, keep your stupid wrist firm," he orders. Then as ball after ball comes over the net, Self 1 reminds Self 2, "Keep it firm. Keep it firm. Keep it firm!" Monotonous? Think how Self 2 must feel! It seems as though Self 1 thinks Self 2 doesn't hear well, or has a short memory, or is stupid. The truth is, of course, that Self 2, which includes the unconscious mind and nervous system, hears everything, never forgets anything, and is anything but stupid. After hitting the ball firmly once, it knows forever which muscles to contract to do it again. That's its nature.

And what's going on during the hit itself? If you look closely at the face of the player, you will see that his cheek muscles are tightening and his lips are pursed in effort and attempted concentration. But tightened face muscles aren't required to hit the backhand, nor do they help concentration. Who's initiating that effort? Self 1, of course. But why? He's supposed to be the teller, not the doer, but it seems he doesn't really trust Self 2 to do the job or else he wouldn't have to do all the work himself. This is the nub of the problem: Self 1 does not trust Self 2, even though it embodies all the potential you have developed up to that moment and is far more competent to control the muscle system than Self 1.

Back to our player. His muscles tense in over-effort, contact is made with the ball, there is a slight flick of the wrist, and the ball hits the back fence. "You bum, you'll never learn how to hit a backhand," Self 1 complains. By thinking too much and trying too hard, Self 1 has produced tension and muscle conflict in the body. He is responsible for the error, but he heaps the blame on Self 2 and then, by condemning it further, undermines his own confidence in Self 2. As a result the stroke grows worse and frustration builds.

"TRYING HARD": A QUESTIONABLE VIRTUE

Haven't we been told since childhood that we're never going to amount to anything unless we try hard? So what does it mean when we observe someone who is trying too hard? Is it best to try medium hard? Equipped with the concept of the two selves, see if you can answer this seeming paradox for yourself after reading the following illustration.

One day while I was wondering about these matters, a very cheery and attractive housewife came to me for a lesson complaining that she was about to give up the game of tennis. She was really very discouraged because, as she said, "I'm really not well coordinated at all. I want to get good enough that my husband will ask me to play mixed doubles with him without making it sound like a family obligation." When I asked her what the problem seemed to be, she said, "For one thing, I can't hit the ball on the strings; most of the time I hit it on the frame."

"Let's take a look," I said, reaching into my basket of balls. I hit her ten waist-high forehands near enough so that she didn't have to move for them. I was surprised that she hit eight out of ten balls either directly on the frame or partly on the strings, partly on the frame. Yet her stroke was good enough. I was puzzled. She hadn't been exaggerating her problem. I wondered if it was her eyesight, but she assured me that her eyes were perfect.

So I told Joan we'd try a few experiments. First I asked her to try very hard to hit the ball on the center of the racket. I was guessing that this might produce even worse results, which would prove my point about trying too hard. But new theories don't always pan out; besides, it takes a lot of talent to hit eight out of ten balls on the narrow frame of a racket. This time, she managed to hit only six balls on the frame. Next, I told her to try to hit the balls on the frame. This time she hit only four on the frame and made good contact with six. She was a bit surprised, but took the chance to give her Self 2 a knock, saying, "Oh, I can never do anything I try to!" Actually, she was close to an important truth. It was becoming clear that her way of trying wasn't helpful.

So before hitting the next set of balls, I asked Joan, "This time I want you to focus your mind on the seams of the ball. Don't think about making contact. In fact, don't try to hit the ball at all. Just *let* your racket contact the ball where *it* wants to, and we'll see what happens." Joan looked more relaxed, and proceeded to hit nine out of ten balls dead center! Only the last ball caught the frame. I asked her if she was aware of what was going through her mind as she swung at the last ball. "Sure," she replied with a lilt in her voice, "I was thinking I might make a tennis player after all." She was right.

Joan was beginning to sense the difference between "trying hard," the energy of Self 1, and "effort," the energy used by Self 2, to do the work necessary. During the last set of balls, Self 1 was fully occupied in watching the seams of the ball. As a result, Self 2 was able to do its own thing unimpaired, and it proved to be pretty good at it. Even Self 1 was starting to recognize the talents of 2; she was getting them together.

Getting it together mentally in tennis involves the learning of several internal skills: 1) learning how to get the clearest possible picture of your desired outcomes; 2) learning how to trust Self 2 to perform at its best and learn from both successes and failures; and 3) learning to see "nonjudgmentally"—that is, to see what is happening rather than merely noticing how well or how badly it is happening. This overcomes "trying too hard." All these skills are subsidiary to the master skill, without which nothing of value is ever achieved: the art of relaxed concentration.

The Inner Game of Tennis will next explore a way to learn these skills, using tennis as a medium.

THREE

Quieting Self 1

WE HAVE ARRIVED AT A KEY POINT: IT IS THE CONSTANT "THINKING" activity of Self 1, the ego-mind, which causes interference with the natural capabilities of Self 2. Harmony between the two selves exists when this mind is quiet and focused. Only then can peak performance be reached.

When a tennis player is "in the zone," he's not thinking about how, when or even where to hit the ball. He's not *trying* to hit the ball, and after the shot he doesn't think about how badly or how well he made contact. The ball seems to get hit through a process which doesn't require thought. There may be an awareness of the sight, sound and feel of the ball, and even of the tactical situation, but the player just seems to *know* without thinking what to do.

Listen to how D. T. Suzuki, a renowned Zen master, de-

scribes the effects of the ego-mind on archery in his foreword to
Zen in the Art of Archery:

> As soon as we reflect, deliberate, and conceptualize, the original
> unconsciousness is lost and a thought interferes. . . . The arrow
> is off the string but does not fly straight to the target, nor does
> the target stand where it is. Calculation, which is miscalculation,
> sets in. . . .
>
> Man is a thinking reed but his great works are done when he is
> not calculating and thinking. "Childlikeness" has to be re-
> stored. . . .

Perhaps this is why it is said that great poetry is born in silence.
Great music and art are said to arise from the quiet depths of the
unconscious, and true expressions of love are said to come from a
source which lies beneath words and thoughts. So it is with the
greatest efforts in sports; they come when the mind is as still as a
glass lake.

Such moments have been called "peak experiences" by the hu-
manistic psychologist Dr. Abraham Maslow. Researching the common characteristics of persons having such experiences, he reports
the following descriptive phrases: "He feels more integrated" [the
two selves are one], "feels at one with the experience," "is relatively
egoless" [quiet mind], "feels at the peak of his powers," "fully functioning," "is in the groove," "effortless," "free of blocks, inhibi-
tions, cautions, fears, doubts, controls, reservations, self-criticisms,
brakes," "he is spontaneous and more creative," "is most here-
now," "is non-striving, non-needing, non-wishing . . . he just is."

If you reflect upon your own highest moments or peak experiences, it is likely that you will recall feelings that these phrases
describe. You will probably also remember them as moments of
great pleasure, even ecstasy. During such experiences, the mind
does not act like a separate entity telling you what you should do
or criticizing how you do it. It is quiet; you are "together," and the
action flows as free as a river.

When this happens on the tennis court, we are focused without *trying* to concentrate. We feel spontaneous and alert. We have an inner assurance that we can do what needs to be done, without having to "try hard." We simply *know* the action will come, and when it does, we don't feel like taking credit; rather, we feel fortunate, "graced." As Suzuki says, we become "childlike."

The image comes to my mind of the balanced movement of a cat stalking a bird. Effortlessly alert, he crouches, gathering his relaxed muscles for the spring. Not thinking about when to jump, nor how he will push off with his hind legs to attain the proper distance, his mind is still and perfectly concentrated on his prey. No thought flashes into his consciousness of the possibility or consequences of missing his mark. He sees only bird. Suddenly the bird takes off; at the same instant, the cat leaps. With perfect anticipation he intercepts his dinner two feet off the ground. Perfectly, thoughtlessly executed action, and afterward, no self-congratulations, just the reward inherent in his action: the bird in the mouth.

In rare moments, tennis players approach the unthinking spontaneity of the leopard. These moments seem to occur most frequently when players are volleying back and forth at the net. Often the exchange of shots at such short quarters is so rapid that action faster than thought is required. These moments are exhilarating, and the players are often amazed to find that they make perfect placements against shots they didn't even expect to reach. Moving more quickly than they thought they could, they have no time to plan; the perfect shot just comes. And feeling that they didn't execute the shot deliberately, they often call it luck; but if it happens repeatedly, one begins to trust oneself and feel a deep sense of confidence.

In short, "getting it together" requires slowing the mind. Quieting the mind means less thinking, calculating, judging, worrying, fearing, hoping, trying, regretting, controlling, jittering or distracting. The mind is still when it is totally here and now in perfect oneness with the action and the actor. It is the purpose of the Inner

Game to increase the frequency and the duration of these moments, quieting the mind by degrees and realizing thereby a continual expansion of our capacity to learn and perform.

At this point the question naturally arises: "How can I quiet Self 1 on the tennis court?" As an experiment the reader might want to put down this book for a minute and simply try to stop thinking. See how long you can remain thoughtless. One minute? Ten seconds? More than likely, you found it difficult, perhaps impossible, to still the mind completely. One thought led to another, then to another, etc.

For most of us, quieting the mind is a gradual process involving the learning of several inner skills. These inner skills are really arts of forgetting mental habits acquired since we were children.

The first skill to learn is the art of letting go the human inclination to judge ourselves and our performance as either good or bad. Letting go of the judging process is a basic key to the Inner Game; its meaning will emerge as you read the remainder of this chapter. When we *un*learn how to be judgmental, it is possible to achieve spontaneous, focused play.

LETTING GO OF JUDGMENTS

To see the process of judgment in action, observe almost any tennis match or lesson. Watch closely the face of the hitter and you will see expressions of judgmental thoughts occurring in his mind. Frowns occur after each "bad" shot, and expressions of self-satisfaction after every shot judged as particularly "good." Often the judgments will be expressed verbally in a vocabulary which ranges widely, depending on the player and the degree of his like or dislike of his shot. Sometimes the judgment is most clearly perceived in the tone of voice used rather than the words themselves. The declaration, "You rolled your racket over again," can be said as a biting self-criticism or a simple observation of fact, depending on the tone of voice. The imperatives, "Watch the ball," or "Move your feet," can be uttered as an encouragement to the body or as a belittling condemnation of its past performance.

To understand more clearly what is meant by judgment, imagine a singles match being played by Mr. A and Mr. B, with Mr. C acting as the umpire. Mr. A is serving his second serve to Mr. B on the first point of a tie-breaker. The ball lands wide, and Mr. C calls, "Out. Double fault." Seeing his serve land out and hearing, "Double fault," Mr. A frowns, says something demeaning about himself, and calls the serve "terrible." Seeing the same stroke, Mr. B. judges it as "good" and smiles. The umpire neither frowns nor smiles; he simply calls the ball as he sees it.

What is important to see here is that neither the "goodness" nor "badness" ascribed to the event by the players is an attribute of the shot itself. Rather, they are evaluations *added* to the event in the minds of the players according to their individual reactions. Mr. A is saying, in effect, "I don't like that event"; Mr. B is saying, "I like that event." The umpire, here ironically called the judge, doesn't judge the event as positive or negative; he simply sees the ball land and calls it out. If the event occurs several more times, Mr. A will get very upset, Mr. B will continue to be pleased, and the umpire, sitting above the scene, will still be noting with detached interest all that is happening.

What I mean by judgment is the act of assigning a negative or positive value to an event. In effect it is saying that some events within your experience are good and you like them, and other events in your experience are bad and you don't like them. You don't like the sight of yourself hitting a ball into the net, but you judge as good the sight of your opponent being aced by your serve. Thus, judgments are our personal, ego reactions to the sights, sounds, feelings and thoughts within our experience.

What does this have to do with tennis? Well, it is the initial act of judgment which provokes a thinking process. First the player's mind judges one of his shots as bad or good. If he judges it as bad, he begins thinking about what was wrong with it. Then he tells himself how to correct it. Then he *tries* hard, giving himself instructions as he does so. Finally he evaluates again. Obviously the mind is anything but still and the body is tight with trying. If the shot is evaluated as good, Self 1 starts wondering how he hit such a good shot; then it tries to get his body to repeat the process by giving self-instructions, trying hard and so on. Both mental processes end in further evaluation, which perpetuates the process of thinking and self-conscious performance. As a consequence, the player's muscles tighten when they need to be loose, strokes become awkward and less fluid, and negative evaluations are likely to continue with growing intensity.

After Self 1 has evaluated several shots, it is likely to start generalizing. Instead of judging a single event as "another bad backhand," it starts thinking, "You have a terrible backhand." Instead of saying, "You were nervous on that point," it generalizes, "You're the worst choke artist in the club." Other common judgmental generalizations are, "I'm having a bad day," "I always miss the easy ones," "I'm slow," etc.

It is interesting to see how the judgmental mind extends itself. It may begin by complaining, "What a lousy serve," then extend to, "I'm serving badly today." After a few more "bad" serves, the judgment may become further extended to "I have a terrible serve." Then, "I'm a lousy tennis player," and finally, "I'm no good." First the mind judges the event, then groups events, then identifies with the combined event and finally judges itself.

As a result, what usually happens is that these self-judgments become self-fulfilling prophecies. That is, they are communications from Self 1 about Self 2 which, after being repeated often enough, become rigidified into expectations or even convictions about Self 2. Then Self 2 begins to live up to these expectations. If you tell yourself often enough that you are a poor server, a kind of hypnotic process takes place. It's as if Self 2 is being given a role to play—the role of bad server—and plays it to the hilt, suppressing for the time being its true capabilities. Once the judgmental mind establishes a self-identity based on its negative judgments, the role-playing continues to hide the true potential of Self 2 until the hypnotic spell is broken. In short, you start to become what you think.

After hitting a number of backhands into the net, the player tells himself that he has a "bad" backhand or at least that his backhand is "off" today. The he goes to the pro to get it fixed much like a sick person goes to a doctor. The pro is then expected to diagnose the faulty backhand and provide the remedy. It all sounds too familiar. In the Chinese tradition of medicine, patients visit their doctors when they are well and the doctor is expected to keep them well. It would be equally possible, and much less frustrating, to approach the tennis pro with your backhand just the way it is without the judgment.

When asked to give up making judgments about one's game, the judgmental mind usually protests, "But if I can't hit a backhand inside the court to save my life, do you expect me to ignore my faults and pretend my game is fine?" Be clear about this: letting go of judgments does not mean ignoring errors. It simply means seeing events as they are and not adding anything to them. Nonjudgmental awareness might observe that during a certain match you hit 50 percent of your first serves into the net. It doesn't ignore the fact. It may accurately describe your serve on that day as erratic and seek to discover the causes. Judgment begins when the serve is labeled "bad" and causes interference with one's playing when a reaction of anger, frustration or discouragement follows. If the judgment process could be stopped with the naming of the event as bad, and there were no further ego reactions, then the interference would be minimal. But judgmental labels usually lead to emotional reactions and then to tightness, trying too hard, self-condemnation, etc. This process can be slowed by using descriptive but nonjudgmental words to describe the events you see.

If a judgmental player comes to me, I will do my best not to believe his tale of a "bad" backhand or of the "bad" player who has it. If he hits the balls out, I will notice they go out, and I may notice the reason why they are going out. But is there a need to judge him or the backhand as sick? If I do, I am likely to get as up-tight in the process of correcting him as he is likely to be in cor-recting himself. Judgment results in tightness, and tightness interferes with the fluidity required for accurate and quick move-ment. Relaxation produces smooth strokes and results from ac-cepting your strokes as they are, even if erratic.

Read this simple analogy and see if an alternative to the judg-ing process doesn't begin to emerge. When we plant a rose seed in the earth, we notice that it is small, but we do not criticize it as "rootless and stemless." We treat it as a seed, giving it the water and nourishment required of a seed. When it first shoots up out of the earth, we don't condemn it as immature and underdeveloped; nor do we criticize the buds for not being open when they appear. We stand in wonder at the process taking place and give the plant the care it needs at each stage of its development. The rose is a rose from the time it is a seed to the time it dies. Within it, at all times, it contains its whole potential. It seems to be constantly in the process of change; yet at each state, at each moment, it is per-fectly all right as it is.

Similarly, the errors we make can be seen as an important part of the developing process. In its process of developing, our tennis game gains a great deal from errors. Even slumps are part of the process. They are not "bad" events, but they seem to endure end-lessly as long as we call them bad and identify with them. Like a good gardener who knows when the soil needs alkali and when acid, the competent tennis pro should be able to help the develop-ment of your game. Usually the first thing that needs to be done is to deal with the negative concepts inhibiting the innate devel-opmental process. Both the pro and the player stimulate this process as they begin to see and to accept the strokes as they are at that moment.

The first step is to see your strokes as they are. They must be per-ceived clearly. This can be done only when personal judgment is absent. As soon as a stroke is seen clearly and accepted as it is, a natural and speedy process of change begins.

The example below, a true story, illustrates the key to un-blocking the natural development in our strokes.

DISCOVERING NATURAL LEARNING

One day in the summer of 1971 when I was teaching a group of men at John Gardiner's Tennis Ranch in Carmel Valley, Califor-nia, a businessman realized how much more power and control he got on his backhand when his racket was taken back below the level of the ball. He was so enthusiastic about his "new" stroke that he rushed to tell his friend Jack about it as if some kind of miracle had occurred. Jack, who considered his erratic backhand one of the major problems of his life, came rushing up to me dur-ing the lunch hour, exclaiming, "I've always had a terrible back-hand. Maybe you can help me."

I asked, "What's so terrible about your backhand?"

"I take my racket back too high on my backswing."

"How do you know?"

"Because at least five different pros have told me so. I just haven't been able to correct it."

For a brief moment I was aware of the absurdity of the situa-tion. Here was a business executive who controlled large com-mercial enterprises of great complexity asking me for help as if he had no control over his own right arm. Why wouldn't it be possi-ble, I wondered, to give him the simple reply, "Sure, I can help you. L-o-w-e-r y-o-u-r r-a-c-k-e-t!"

But complaints such as Jack's are common among people of all levels of intelligence and proficiency. Besides, it was clear that at least five other pros had told him to lower his racket without much effect. What was keeping him from doing it? I wondered.

I asked Jack to take a few swings on the patio where we were standing. His backswing started back very low, but then, sure enough, just before swinging forward it lifted to the level of his shoulder and swung down into the imagined ball. The five pros were right. I asked him to swing several more times without making any comment. "Isn't that better?" he asked. "I tried to keep it low." But each time just before swinging forward, his racket lifted; it was obvious that had he been hitting an actual ball, the underspin imparted by the downward swing would have caused it to sail out.

"Your backhand is all right," I said reassuringly. "It's just going through some changes. Why don't you take a closer look at it." We walked over to a large windowpane and there I asked him to swing again while watching his reflection. He did so, again taking his characteristic hitch at the back of his swing, but this time he was astounded. "Hey, I really do take my racket back high! It goes up above my shoulder!" There was no judgment in his voice; he was just reporting with amazement what his eyes had seen.

What surprised me was Jack's surprise. Hadn't he said that five pros had told him his racket was too high? I was certain that if I had told him the same thing after his first swing, he would have replied, "Yes, I know." But what was now clear was that he didn't *really* know, since no one is ever surprised at seeing something they already know. Despite all those lessons, he had never *directly* experienced his racket going back high. His mind had been so absorbed in the process of judgment and trying to change this "bad" stroke that he had never perceived the stroke itself.

Looking in the glass which mirrored his stroke as it was, Jack was able to keep his racket low quite effortlessly as he swung again. "That feels entirely different than any backhand I've ever swung," he declared. By now he was swinging up and through the ball over and over again. Interestingly, he wasn't congratulating himself for doing it right; he was simply absorbed in how different it *felt*.

After lunch I threw Jack a few balls and he was able to remember how the stroke felt and to repeat the action. This time he just felt where his racket was going, letting his sense of feel replace the visual image offered by the mirror. It was a new experience for him. Soon he was consistently hitting topspin backhands into the court with an effortlessness that made it appear this was his natural swing. In ten minutes he was feeling "in the groove," and he paused to express his gratitude. "I can't tell you how much I ap-

preciate what you've done for me. I've learned more in ten minutes from you than in twenty hours of lessons I've taken on my
backhand." I could feel something inside me begin to puff up as it
absorbed these "good" words. At the same time, I didn't know
quite how to handle this lavish compliment, and found myself
hemming and hawing, trying to come up with an appropriately
modest reply. Then, for a moment, my mind turned off and I realized that I hadn't given Jack a single instruction on his backhand! "But what did I teach you?" I asked. He was quiet for a full
half-minute, trying to remember what I had told him. Finally he
said, "I can't remember your telling me anything! You were just
there watching, and you got me watching myself closer than I
ever had before. Instead of seeing what was *wrong* with my backhand, I just started observing, and improvement seemed to happen on its own. I'm not sure why, but I certainly learned a lot in a
short period of time." He had learned, but had he been "taught"?
This question fascinated me.

I can't describe how good I felt at that moment, or why. Tears
even began to come to my eyes. I had learned and he had learned,
but there was no one there to take credit. There was only the
glimmer of a realization that we were *both* participating in a wonderful process of natural learning.

The key that unlocked Jack's new backhand—which was
really there all the time just waiting to be let out—was that in the
instant he stopped trying to change his backhand, he saw it as it
was. At first, with the aid of the mirror, he directly *experienced* his
backswing. Without thinking or analyzing, he increased his
awareness of that part of his swing. When the mind is free of any
thought or judgment, it is still and acts like a mirror. Then and
only then can we know things as they are.

AWARENESS OF WHAT IS

In the game of tennis there are two important things to know.
The first is where the ball is. The second is where the racket head

is. From the time anyone begins to learn tennis, he is told the importance of watching the ball. It's very simple: you come to know where the ball is by looking at it. You don't have to think, "Oh, here comes the ball; it's clearing the net by about one foot and coming pretty fast. It should bounce near the baseline, and I'd better hit it on the rise." No, you simply watch the ball and let the proper response take place.

In the same way, you don't have to think about where your racket head *should* be, but you should realize the importance of being aware of where the racket head *is* at all times. You can't look at it to know where it is because you're watching the ball. You must *feel* it. Feeling it gives you the knowledge of where it is. Knowing where it *should be* isn't feeling where it is. Knowing what your racket *didn't do* isn't feeling where it is. *Feeling* where it is is *knowing* where it is.

No matter what a person's complaint when he has a lesson with me, I have found that the most beneficial first step is to encourage him to *see* and *feel* what he is doing—that is, to increase his awareness of *what actually is*. I follow the same process when my own strokes get out of their groove. But to see things as they are, we must take off our judgmental glasses, whether they're dark or rose-tinted. This action unlocks a process of natural development which is as surprising as it is beautiful.

For example, suppose that a player complains that the timing on his forehand is off. I wouldn't give him an analysis of what is wrong and then instruct him, "Take your racket back sooner," or "Hit the ball farther out in front of you." Instead I might simply ask him to put his attention on where his racket head is at the moment the ball bounces on his side of the net. Since this is not a common instruction, it is likely that the player will never have been told anything about where his racket should or shouldn't be at that particular moment. If his judgmental mind is engaged, he is likely to become a little nervous, since Self 1 likes to try to do things "right" and is nervous when he doesn't know the rightness or wrongness of a particular action. So at once the player may ask where his racket should be when the ball is bouncing. But I decline to say, asking him only to observe where his racket *is* at that moment.

After he hits a few balls, I ask him to tell me where his racket was at the moment in question. The typical reply is, "I'm taking my racket back too late. I know what I'm doing wrong, but I can't stop it." This is a common response of players of all sports, and is the cause of a great deal of frustration.

"Forget about right and wrong for now," I suggest. "Just observe your racket at the moment of bounce." After five or ten more balls are hit to him, the player is likely to reply, "I'm doing better; I'm getting it back earlier."

"Yes, and where was your racket?" I ask.

"I don't know, but I think I was getting it back on time . . . wasn't I?"

Uncomfortable without a standard for right and wrong, the judgmental mind makes up standards of its own. Meanwhile, attention is taken off what *is* and placed on the process of trying to do things right. Even though he may be getting his racket back earlier and is hitting the ball more solidly, he is still in the dark about where his racket is. (If the player is left in this state, thinking that he has found the "secret" to his problem—that is, getting his racket back earlier—he will be momentarily pleased. He will go out eagerly to play and repeat to himself before hitting every forehand, "Get it back early, get it back early, get it back early . . ." For a while this magic phrase will seem to produce "good" results. But after a while, he will start missing again in spite of his self-reminder, will wonder what's going "wrong" and will come back to the pro for another tip.)

So instead of stopping the process at the point where the player is judging positively, I again ask him to observe his racket and to tell me exactly where it is at the moment of bounce. As the player finally lets himself observe his racket with detachment and interest, he can feel what it is actually doing and his awareness increases. Then, without any effort to correct, he will discover that his swing has begun to develop a natural rhythm. In fact, he will find the best rhythm for himself, which may be slightly different from what might be dictated by some universal standard called "correct." Then when he goes out to play, he has no magic phrase that must be repeated, and can focus without thinking.

What I have tried to illustrate is that there is a natural learning process which operates within everyone—if it is allowed to. This process is waiting to be discovered by all those who do not know of its existence. There is no need to take my word for it; it can be discovered for yourself if it hasn't been already. If it has been experienced, trust it. (This is the subject of chapter 4.) To discover this natural learning process, it is necessary to let go of the old process of *correcting* faults; that is, it is necessary to let go of judgment and see what happens. Will your strokes develop under the effect of noncritical attention or won't they? Test this.

WHAT ABOUT POSITIVE THINKING?

Before finishing with the subject of the judgmental mind, something needs to be said about "positive thinking." The "bad" effects of negative thinking are frequently discussed these days. Books and articles advise readers to replace negative thinking with positive thinking. People are advised to stop telling themselves they are ugly, uncoordinated, unhappy or whatever, and to repeat to themselves that they are attractive, well coordinated and happy. The substituting of a kind of "positive hypnotism" for a previous habit of "negative hypnotism" may appear at least to have short-range benefits, but I have always found that the honeymoon ends all too soon.

One of the first lessons I learned as a teaching pro was not to find fault with any pupil or even his strokes. So I stopped criticizing either. Instead, I would compliment the pupil when I could, and make only positive suggestions about how to correct his strokes. Some time later, I found myself no longer complimenting my students. The realization that preceded this change occurred one day when I was giving a group of women a lesson on footwork.

I had made a few introductory remarks about self-criticism when Clare, one of the women, asked, "I can understand that negative thinking is harmful, but what about complimenting yourself when you do well? What about positive thinking?" My answer to her was vague—"Well, I don't think positive thinking is as harmful as negative thinking"—but during the lesson that followed, I came to see the issue more clearly.

At the beginning of the lesson, I told the women that I was going to hit each of them six running forehands, and that I wanted them simply to become aware of their feet. "Get in touch with how your feet move getting into position, and whether there is any transfer of weight as you hit the ball." I told them that there was no right and wrong to think about; they were only to observe their own footwork with full attention. While I hit the balls to them, I made no comments. I watched intently what was happening before my eyes, but expressed no judgment either positive or negative. Similarly, the women were quiet, watching each other without comment. They each seemed absorbed in the simple process of experiencing the movement of their feet.

After the series of thirty balls, I noticed that there were no balls at the net; they were all bunched together in the crosscourt area on my side. "Look," I said, "all the balls are together in the corner, and not one at the net." Although semantically this remark was simply an observation of fact, my tone of voice revealed that I was pleased with what I saw. I was complimenting them, and indirectly I was complimenting myself as their instructor.

To my surprise, the girl who was due to hit next said, "Oh, you would have to say that just before my turn!" Though she was half kidding, I could see that she was a little nervous. I repeated the same instructions as before and hit thirty more balls without comment. This time there were frowns appearing on the women's

faces and their footwork seemed a little more awkward than before. After the thirtieth ball, there were eight balls at the net and
the balls behind me were quite scattered.

Inwardly I criticized myself for having spoiled the magic.
Then Clare, the girl who had originally asked me about positive
thinking, exclaimed, "Oh, I ruined it for everyone. I was the first
to hit a ball into the net, and I hit four of them." I was amazed, as
were the others, because it wasn't true. It was another person who
had netted the first ball, and Clare had hit only two balls into the
net. Her judgmental mind had distorted her perception of what
had actually happened.

Then I asked the women if they were aware of something different going through their minds during the second series of
balls. Each of them reported being less aware of their feet and
more intent on trying to keep from hitting balls into the net.
They were trying to live up to an expectation, a standard of right
and wrong, which they felt had been set before them. This was exactly what had been missing during the first set of balls. I began to
see that my compliment had engaged their judgmental minds.
Self 1, the ego-mind, had gotten into the act.

Through this experience, I began to see how Self 1 operated.
Always looking for approval and wanting to avoid disapproval,
this subtle ego-mind sees a compliment as a potential criticism. It
reasons, "If the pro is pleased with one kind of performance, he
will be displeased by the opposite. If he likes me for doing well, he
will dislike me for not doing well." The standard of good and bad
had been established, and the inevitable result was divided concentration and ego-interference.

The women also began to realize the cause of their tightness
on the third round of balls. Then Clare seemed to light up like a
1000-watt bulb. "Oh, I see!" she exclaimed, slapping her hand to
her forehead. "My compliments are criticisms in disguise. I use
both to manipulate behavior." Whereupon she ran off the court
saying she had to find her husband. Evidently she had seen connection between how she treated herself on the tennis court and

her family relationships, for an hour later I saw her with her husband, still absorbed in intense conversation.

Clearly, positive and negative evaluations are relative to each other. It is impossible to judge one event as positive without seeing other events as not positive or as negative. There is no way to stop just the negative side of the judgmental process. To see your strokes as they are, there is no need to attribute goodness or badness to them. The same goes for the results of your strokes. You can notice exactly how far out a ball lands without labeling it a "bad" event. By ending judgment, you do not avoid seeing what is. Ending judgment means you neither add nor subtract from the facts before your eyes. Things appear as they are—undistorted. In this way, the mind becomes more calm.

"But," protests Self 1, "if I see my ball going out and I don't evaluate it as bad, I won't have any incentive to change it. If I don't dislike what I'm doing wrong, how am I going to change it?" Self 1, the ego-mind, wants to take responsibility for making things "better." It wants the credit for playing an important role in things. It also worries and suffers a lot when things don't go its way.

The following chapter will deal with an alternative process: a process by which actions flow spontaneously and sensibly without an ego-mind on the scene chasing positives and trying to reform negatives. But before concluding this chapter, read this profound but deceptively simple story told me by a much respected friend of mine named Bill.

Three men in a car are driving down a city street early one morning. For the sake of analogy, suppose that each man represents a different kind of tennis player. The man sitting on the right is a positive thinker who believes that his game is great and is full of self-esteem because his tennis is so superior. He's also a self-admitted playboy who enjoys all "the pleasures" life has to offer. The man sitting in the middle is a negative thinker who is constantly analyzing what is wrong with himself and the world. He is always involved in some kind of self-improvement program. The third man, who is driving, is in the process of letting go of judgmental thinking altogether. He plays the Inner Game, enjoying things as they are and doing what seems sensible.

The car pulls up at a stoplight, and crossing the street in front of the car is a beautiful young lady who catches the attention of all three men. Her beauty is particularly apparent as she is stark naked!

The man on the right becomes engrossed in thoughts of how nice it would be to be with this lady under other circumstances. His mind races through past memories and future fantasies of sensual pleasures.

The man sitting in the middle is seeing an example of modern decadence. He's not sure that he should be looking closely at the girl. First miniskirts, he thinks, then topless dancers, then bottomless dancers, and now they're out on the streets in broad daylight! Something must be done to stop all this!

The driver is seeing the same girl that the others are observing, but is simply watching what is before his eyes. He sees neither good nor bad, and as a result, a detail comes to his attention which was not noticed by either of his companions: the girl's eyes are shut. He realizes that the lady is sleepwalking. Responding immediately with common sense, he asks the person next to him to take the wheel, steps out of the car, and puts his overcoat over the woman's shoulders. He gently wakes her and explains to her that she must have been sleepwalking and offers to take her home.

My friend Bill used to end the story with a twinkle in his eye, saying, "There he received the rewards of his action," leaving each listener to hear what he would.

THE FIRST INNER SKILL to be developed in the Inner Game is that of nonjudgmental awareness. When we "unlearn" judgment we discover, usually with some surprise, that we don't need the motivation of a reformer to change our "bad" habits. We may simply need to be more aware. There is a more natural process of learning and performing waiting to be discovered. It is waiting to show what it can do when allowed to operate without interference from the conscious strivings of the judgmental self. The discovery of and reliance upon this process is the subject of the next chapter.

But first, one balancing thought. It is important to remember that not all remarks are judgmental. *Acknowledgment* of one's own or another's strengths, efforts, accomplishments, etc., can facilitate natural learning, whereas judgments interfere. What is the difference? Acknowledgment of and respect for one's capabilities support trust in Self 2. Self 1's judgments, on the other hand, attempt to manipulate and undermine that trust.

FOUR

Trusting Self 2

THE THESIS OF THE LAST CHAPTER WAS THAT THE FIRST STEP IN bringing a greater harmony between ego-mind and body—that is, between Self 1 and Self 2—was to let go of self-judgment. Only when Self 1 stops sitting in judgment over Self 2 and its actions can he become aware of who and what Self 2 is and appreciate the processes by which it works. As this step occurs, trust is developed, and eventually the basic but elusive ingredient for all top performance emerges—self-confidence.

WHO AND WHAT IS SELF 2?

Put aside for a moment the opinions you have about your body—whether you think of it as clumsy, uncoordinated, average or really fantastic—and think about what it does. As you read these very words your body is performing a remarkable piece of coordination. Eyes are moving effortlessly, taking in images of black and white which are automatically compared with memories of similar markings, translated into symbols, then connected with other symbols to form an impression of meaning. Thousands of these operations are taking place every few seconds. At the same time, again without conscious effort, your heart is pumping and your breath is going in and out, keeping a fantastically complicated system of organs, glands and muscles nourished and working. Without conscious effort, billions of cells are functioning, reproducing and fighting off disease.

If you walked to a chair and turned on a light before beginning to read, your body coordinated a great number of muscle movements to accomplish those tasks. Self 1 did not have to tell your body how far to reach before closing your fingers on the light switch; you knew your goal, and your body did what was necessary without thought. The process by which the body learned and performed these actions is no different from the process by which it learns and plays the game of tennis.

Reflect on the complicated series of actions performed by Self 2 in the process of returning a serve. In order to anticipate how and where to move the feet and whether to take the racket back on the forehand or backhand side, the brain must calculate within a fraction of a second the moment the ball leaves the server's racket approximately where it is going to land and where the racket will intercept it. Into this calculation must be computed the initial velocity of the ball, combined with an input for the progressive decrease in velocity and the effect of wind and of spin, to say nothing of the complicated trajectories involved. Then, each of these factors must be recalculated after the bounce of the ball to anticipate the point where contact will be made by the racket. Simultaneously, muscle orders must be given—not just once, but constantly refined on updated information. Finally, the muscles have to respond in cooperation with one another: a movement of feet occurs, the racket is taken back at a certain speed and height, and the face of the racket is kept at a constant angle as the racket and body move forward in balance. Contact is made at a precise point according to whether the order was given to hit down the line or cross-court—an order not given until after a split-second analysis of the movement and balance of the opponent on the other side of the net.

If Pete Sampras is serving, you have less than half a second to accomplish all this. Even if you are returning the serve of an average player, you will have only about one second. Just to hit the ball is clearly a remarkable feat; to return it with consistency and accuracy is a mind-boggling achievement. Yet it is not uncommon. The truth is that everyone who inhabits a human body possesses a remarkable instrument.

In the light of this, it seems inappropriate to call our bodies derogatory names. Self 2—that is, the physical body, including the brain, memory bank (conscious and unconscious) and the nervous system—is a tremendously sophisticated and competent collection of potentialities. Inherent within it is an inner intelligence which is staggering. What it doesn't already know, this inner intelligence learns with childlike ease. It uses billions of cells and neurological communication circuits in every action. No computer yet made can come close to performing the complex physical actions accomplished by even a beginning tennis player, much less a professional.

The foregoing has only one purpose: to encourage the reader to respect Self 2. This amazing instrument is what we have the effrontery to call "uncoordinated."

Reflect on the silent intelligence inherent in all Self 2 actions and our attitude of arrogance and mistrust will gradually change. With it will dissolve the unnecessary self-instructions, criticisms and tendencies to overcontrol that tend to occupy the unfocused mind.

TRUST THYSELF

As long as Self 1 is either too ignorant or too proud to acknowledge the capabilities of Self 2, true self-confidence will be hard to come by. It is Self 1's mistrust of Self 2 which causes both the interference called "trying too hard" and that of too much self-instruction. The first results in using too many muscles, the second in mental distraction and lack of concentration. Clearly, the new relationship to be established with ourselves must be based on the maxim "Trust thyself."

What does "Trust thyself" mean on the tennis court? It doesn't mean positive thinking—for example, expecting that you are going to hit an ace on every serve. Trusting your body in tennis means *letting* your body hit the ball. The key word is *let*. You trust in the competence of your body and its brain, and you *let* it swing the racket. Self 1 stays out of it. But though this is very simple, it does not mean that it is easy.

In some ways the relationship between Self 1 and Self 2 is analogous to the relationship between parent and child. Some parents have a hard time letting their children do something when they believe that they themselves know better how it should be done. But the trusting and loving parent lets the child perform his own actions, even to the extent of making mistakes, because he trusts the child to learn from them.

Letting it happen is not *making* it happen. It is not *trying* hard. It is not controlling your shots. These are all the actions of Self 1, which takes things into its own hands because it mistrusts Self 2. This is what produces tight muscles, rigid swings, awkward movements, gritted teeth and tense cheek muscles. The results are mis-hit balls and a lot of frustration. Often when we are rallying we trust our bodies and let it happen because the ego-mind tells itself that it doesn't really count. But once the game begins, watch Self 1 take over; at the crucial point it starts to doubt whether Self 2 will perform well. The more important the point, the more Self 1 may try to control the shot, and this is exactly when tightening up occurs. The results are almost always frustrating.

Let's take a closer look at this tightening process, because it is a phenomenon which takes place in every athlete in every sport. Anatomy tells us that muscles are two-way mechanisms; that is, a given muscle is either relaxed or contracted. It can't be partially contracted any more than a light switch can be partially off. The difference between holding our racket loosely or tightly is in the *number* of muscles which are contracted. How many and which muscles are actually needed to hit a fast serve? No one knows, but if the conscious mind *thinks* it does and tries to control those muscles, it will inevitably use muscles that aren't needed. When more than necessary are used, not only is there a waste of energy, but certain tightened muscles interfere with the need of other muscles to relax. Thinking that it has to use a lot of muscle to hit as hard as it wants to, Self 1 will initiate the use of muscles in the shoulder, forearm, wrist and even face which will actually *impede* the force of the swing.

If you have a racket handy, hold it and try this experiment. (If you don't have a racket, grab any movable object, or just grab the air with your hand.) Tighten up the muscles in your wrist and see how fast you can snap your racket. Then release the muscles in your wrist and see how fast it will snap. Clearly, a loose wrist is more flexible. When serving, power is generated, at least in part, by the flexible snap of the wrist. If you try to hit hard intentionally, you are likely to over-tighten the wrist muscles, slow down the snap of your wrist and thereby lose power. Furthermore, the entire stroke will be rigid, and balance will be difficult to maintain. This is how Self 1 interferes with the wisdom of the body. (As you can imagine, a stiff-wristed serve will not meet the expectations of the server. Consequently he is likely to try even harder next time, tightening more muscles, and becoming more and more frustrated and exhausted—and, I might add, increasing the risk of tennis elbow.)

Fortunately, most children learn to walk before they can be told how to by their parents. Yet, children not only learn how to walk very well, but they gain confidence in the natural learning process which operates within them. Mothers observe their children's efforts with love and interest, and if they are wise, without much interference. If we could treat our tennis games as we do a child learning to walk, we would make more progress. When the child loses his balance and falls, the mother doesn't condemn it for being clumsy. She doesn't even feel bad about it; she simply notices the event and perhaps gives a word or gesture of encouragement. Consequently, a child's progress in learning to walk is never hindered by the idea that he is uncoordinated.

Why shouldn't a beginning player treat his backhand as a loving mother would her child? The trick is not to *identify* with the backhand. If you view an erratic backhand as a reflection of who you are, you will be upset. But you are not your backhand any more than a parent is his child. If a mother identifies with every fall of her child and takes personal pride in its every success, her self-image will be as unstable as her child's balance. She finds stability when she realizes that she is not her child, and watches it with love and interest—but as a separate being.

This same kind of detached interest is what is necessary to let your tennis game develop naturally. Remember that you are not your tennis game. You are not your body. Trust the body to learn and to play, as you would trust another person to do a job, and in a short time it will perform beyond your expectations. *Let* the flower grow.

The preceding theory should be tested and not taken on faith. Toward the end of the chapter there are several experiments that will give you a chance to experience the difference between *making* yourself do something, and *letting* it happen. I suggest that you also devise your own experiments to discover just how much you are willing to trust yourself, both when rallying and when under pressure.

LET IT HAPPEN

At this point it may have occurred to the reader to ask, "How can I just 'let a forehand happen' if I've never learned how to hit one in the first place? Don't I need someone to tell me how to do it? If I've never played tennis before, can I just go out on the court and 'let it happen'?" The answer is: if your body knows how to hit a forehand, then just *let it happen*; if it doesn't, then *let it learn*.

The actions of Self 2 are based on information it has stored in its memory of past actions of itself or of the observed actions of others. A player who has never held a racket in his hand needs to let the ball hit the strings a few times before Self 2 learns how far away the center of the racket is from the hand holding it. Every time you hit a ball, whether correctly or incorrectly, the computer memory of Self 2 is picking up valuable information and storing it away for future use. As one practices, Self 2 refines and extends the information in its memory bank. All the time it is learning such things as how high a ball bounces when hit at varying speeds and varying spins; how fast a ball falls and how fast it comes up off the court; and where it should be met to direct it to different parts of the court. It remembers every action it makes and the results of every action, depending on the degree of your attention and alertness. So the important thing for a beginning player to remember is to allow the natural learning process to take place and to forget about stroke-by-stroke self-instructions. The results will be surprising.

Let me illustrate with an example which demonstrates the easy and hard ways of learning. When I was twelve years old, I was sent to dancing school, where I was taught the waltz, fox trot and other steps known only to the darker ages of man. We were told, "Put your right foot here and your left foot there, then bring them together. Now shift your weight to your left foot, turn," and so forth. The steps were not complicated, but it was weeks before I was dancing without the need to play back the tape in my head: "Put your left foot here, right foot there, turn, one, two, three; one, two, three." I would think out each step, command myself to do it and then execute it. I was barely aware there was a girl in my arms, and it was weeks before I was able to handle a conversation while dancing.

This is the way most of us teach ourselves the footwork and strokes of tennis. But it's such a slow and painful way! Contrast it with the way the modern twelve-year-old learns to dance. He goes to a party one night, sees his friends doing whatever dances are in vogue at the time, and comes home having mastered them all. Yet these dances are infinitely more complex than the fox trot. Just imagine the size of the instruction manual required to put into words each of the movements of these dances! It would require a Ph.D. in physical education and a full semester to learn them "by the book." But a kid who may be failing math and English learns them effortlessly in a single night.

How does he do this? First, by simply *watching*. He doesn't think about what he is seeing—how the left shoulder lifts a bit while the head jerks forward and the right foot twists. He simply absorbs *visually* the image in front of him. This image completely bypasses the ego-mind, and seems to be fed directly to the body, for in a few minutes the kid is on the floor doing movements very similar to those he was watching. Now he is *feeling* how it is to imitate those images. He repeats the process a few times, first looking, then feeling, and soon is dancing effortlessly—totally "with it." If the next day he is asked by his sister how to do the dance he'll say, "I don't know . . . like this . . . see?" Ironically, he thinks he doesn't know how to do the dance because he can't explain it in words, while most of us who learn tennis through verbal instruction can explain in great detail how the ball should be hit but have trouble *doing* it.

To Self 2, a picture is worth a thousand words. It learns by watching the actions of others, as well as by performing actions itself. Almost all tennis players have experienced playing over their heads after watching championship tennis on television. The benefits to your game come not from analyzing the strokes of top players, but from concentrating without thinking and simply letting yourself absorb the images before you. Then, the next time you play, you may find that certain important intangibles such as timing, anticipation and sense of confidence are greatly improved, all without conscious effort or control.

COMMUNICATING WITH SELF 2

In short, for many of us, a new relationship needs to be forged with Self 2. And building new relationships involves new ways of communicating. If the former relationship was characterized by criticism and control, the symptoms of mistrust, then the more desired relationship is one of respect and trust. If so, this change can start with a change of *attitude*. If you observe Self 1, in its critical posture, it looks *down* at Self 2 and diminishes it (in its own eyes) with its disparaging thoughts. The other possibility is to learn to look *up* to Self 2. This is the attitude of respect based on true recognition of its natural intelligence and capabilities. Another word for this attitude is humility, a feeling that happens naturally in the presence of something or someone you admire. As you find your way to an attitude that slopes upward toward Self 2 with respect, the feelings and thoughts that accompany the controlling and critical attitude fade and the sincerity of Self 2 emerges. With an attitude of respect, you learn to speak in the language of the respected person.

The remainder of this chapter will discuss three basic methods of communicating with Self 2. It is basic to good communications that we use the most suitable language. If Mr. A wishes to make sure of getting his message across to Mr. B, he will, if he can, use Mr. B's native tongue. What is the native language of Self 2? Certainly not words! Words were not learned by Self 2 until several years after birth. No, the native tongue of Self 2 is imagery: sensory images. Movements are learned through visual and feeling images. So the three methods of communicating I will discuss all involve sending goal-oriented messages to Self 2 by images and "feelmages."

ASKING FOR RESULTS

Many students of tennis are too stroke-conscious and not attentive enough to results. Such players are aware of *how* they stroke the ball, but unconcerned with *where* it is actually going. It is often helpful for these players to shift their attention from means to ends. Here is an example.

During a group lesson with five women, I asked each player

what one change she would most like to make in her game. The first woman, Sally, wanted to work on her forehand, which she said "had really been terrible lately." When I asked her what she didn't like about her forehand, she replied, "Well, I take my racket back too late and too high, and I roll it over too much on the follow-through; also I take my eye off the ball a lot, and I don't think I step into it very well." It was clear that if I were to give her instruction on each element she mentioned, I would start and end the lesson with her.

So I asked Sally what she felt about the results of her fore-hand, and she replied, "It goes too shallow and doesn't have much power." Now we had something we could work with. I told her that I imagined her body (Self 2) already knew how to hit the ball deep and with more power, and that if it didn't, it would learn very quickly. I suggested that she imagine the arc the ball would have to take to land deep in the court, noticing how high over the net it would pass, and hold that image in her mind for several seconds. Then, before hitting some balls, I said, "Don't *try* to hit the ball deep. Just ask Self 2 to do it and let it happen. If the ball contin-ues to fall shallow, don't make any conscious effort to correct. Simply let go and see what happens."

The third ball Sally hit landed a foot inside the baseline. Of the next twenty, fifteen landed in the back quarter of the court and did so with increasing force behind them. As she hit, the other four women and I could see all the elements she had mentioned changing appreciably and naturally; her backswing lowered, her follow-through flattened, and she began flowing into the ball with balance and confidence. When she was finished hitting, I asked her what changes she had made, and she replied, "I didn't make any. I just imagined the ball passing two feet over the net and landing near the baseline, and it did!" She was both delighted and surprised.

The changes that Sally made in her forehand lay in the fact that she gave Self 2 a clear visual image of the *results* she desired.

Then she told her body in effect, "Do whatever you have to do to go there." All she had to do was *let it happen.*

Getting the clearest possible image of your desired outcomes is a most useful method for communicating with Self 2, especially when playing a match. Once you are competing it is too late to work on your strokes, but it is possible to hold in your mind the image of where you want the ball to go and then allow the body to do what is necessary to hit it there. It is essential here to trust Self 2. Self 1 must stay relaxed, refraining from giving "how-to-do-it" instructions and from any effort to control the stroke. As Self 1 learns to let go, a growing confidence in the ability of Self 2 emerges.

ASKING FOR FORM

It is sometimes useful to be able to make a deliberate change in one or more elements of a given stroke. (This process will be discussed in greater detail in chapter 6, "Changing Habits.")

In brief, the process is very similar to asking for results. Suppose, for example, that you are consistently rolling your racket over on the follow-through, and the habit continues despite all efforts to change it. First you must give Self 2 a very clear image of what you are asking it to do. This can best be done by holding your racket in front of you in a proper follow-through position and looking at it with undivided attention for several seconds. You may feel foolish, thinking that you already know the proper follow-through, but it is vital to give Self 2 an image to imitate. Having done this, it might also be useful to shut your eyes and imagine as clearly as possible your entire forehand with the racket staying flat throughout the swing. Then, before hitting any balls, swing your racket several times, letting the racket stay flat and allowing yourself to experience how it feels to swing in this new way. Once you start to hit balls, it is important not to try and keep your racket flat. You have asked Self 2 to keep it flat, so *let it happen!*

Self 1's only role is to be still and observe the results in a detached manner. Let me stress again that it is important not to make any conscious effort to keep the racket flat. If after a few strokes the racket does not conform to the image you gave Self 2, then image the desired outcome again and let your body swing your racket, making sure Self 2 isn't giving it the slightest assistance. Don't *try* to make this experiment work; if you do, Self 1 will get involved and you won't really know if Self 2 is hitting the ball unassisted or not.

TWO EXPERIMENTS

It is important not only to understand intellectually the difference between *letting* it happen and *making* it happen, but to *experience* the difference. To experience the difference is to know the difference. To this end, let me suggest two experiments.

The first involves trying to hit a stationary target with a tennis ball. Place a tennis-ball can in the backhand corner of one of the service courts. Then figure out how you should swing your racket in order to hit the can. Think about how high to toss the ball, about the proper angle of your racket at impact, the proper weight flow and so forth. Now aim at the can and attempt to hit it. If you miss, try again. If you hit it, try to repeat whatever you did so that you can hit it again. If you follow this procedure for a few minutes, you will experience what I mean by "trying hard" and *making* yourself serve.

After you have absorbed this experience, move the can to the backhand corner of the other service court for the second half of the experiment. This time stand on the baseline, breathe deeply a few times and relax. Look at the can. Then visualize the path of the ball from your racket to the can. See the ball hitting the can right on the label. If you like, shut your eyes and imagine yourself serving and the ball hitting the can. Do this several times. If in your imagination the ball misses the can, that's all right; repeat the image a few times until the ball hits the target. Now, take no thought of how you should hit the ball. Don't *try* to hit the target. *Ask* your body, Self 2, to do whatever is necessary to hit the can, then let it do it. Exercise no control; correct for no imagined bad habits. Simply trust your body to do it. When you toss the ball up, focus your attention on its seams, then let the serve serve itself.

The ball will either hit or miss the target. Notice exactly where it lands. You should free yourself from any emotional reaction to success or failure; simply know your goal and take objective interest in the results. Then serve again. If you have missed the can, don't be surprised and don't try to correct for your error. This is most important. Again focus your attention on the can; then let the serve serve itself. If you faithfully do not *try* to hit the can, and do not attempt to correct for your misses, but put full confidence in your body and its computer, you will soon see that the serve is correcting itself. You will experience that there really is a Self 2 who is acting and learning without being told what to do. Observe this process; observe your body making the changes necessary in order to come nearer and nearer to the can. Of course, Self 1 is very tricky and it is most difficult to keep it from interfering a little, but if you quiet it a bit, you will begin to see Self 2 at work, and you will be as amazed as I have been at what it can do, and how effortlessly.

The second experiment I would recommend in order to experience the reality of Self 2 begins with picking some change you would like to make in one of your strokes. For instance, choose a bad habit that you have been trying unsuccessfully to alter. Then on the court, ask a friend to throw you twenty balls and try to correct the habit. Tell him what you are trying to do and ask him to observe if it is correcting. Try hard; try the way you are used to in attempting to change a habit. Experience this kind of trying. Observe how you feel if you fail. Also note whether you feel awkward or tight. Now try to practice your corrected stroke while rallying. Then see what happens when you play a match.

Next, pick another habit you would like to change, or even the same one. (If the habit has not been corrected by your first efforts, it would be interesting to work on the same one.) Ask your friend to throw you five or ten balls. During this, make no attempt to change your stroke; simply observe it. Don't analyze it, just *observe* it carefully; experience where your racket is at all times. Changes may occur while you are merely observing your stroke nonjudgmentally, but if you feel further correction is needed, then "create an image of the desired form." Show yourself exactly what you want Self 2 to do. Give it a clear visual image, moving your racket slowly in the desired path, and let yourself watch it very closely. Then repeat the process, but this time *feel* exactly what it's like to move your racket in this new manner.

Having provided yourself with an image and a feeling, you are ready to hit some balls. Now focus your eyes and mind on the seams of the ball and *let it happen*. Then *observe* what happened. Once again, don't analyze; simply see how close Self 2 came to doing what you wanted it to. If your racket didn't follow the path you had imaged, then re-create the image and let the stroke happen again. Continue this process, letting Self 1 relax more and more with each ball. Soon you will see that Self 2 can be trusted. Long-standing habits can be altered in a few moments. After twenty balls or so, ask your friend to rally again with you. Be sure you don't try to make this experiment work by attempting to do it "right" when playing; merely continue to observe the precise part of your swing that is changing. Watch it with detachment and care as you would watch someone else's stroke. Watch it, and it will change quite effortlessly by its own smooth process.

Perhaps this seems too good to be true. I can only suggest that you experiment and see for yourself.

More needs to be said about this art of changing habits because it is what so many players spend so much time and money on in lessons, but before undertaking a fuller description of this art, let's discuss a third method of communicating with Self 2.

ASKING FOR QUALITIES

In the last chapter, I pointed out how the process of judgment often feeds on and extends itself until a strong negative self-image has formed. One begins believing that he is not a good tennis player and then acts this role, never allowing himself anything but glimpses of his true capabilities. Most players hypnotize themselves into acting the roles of much worse players than they actually are, but interesting results can often be achieved by doing a little role-playing of a different kind.

"Asking for qualities" describes this other kind of role-playing. When introducing this idea, I usually say something like this: "Imagine that I am the director of a television series. Knowing that you are an actor that plays tennis, I ask if you would like to do a bit part as a top-flight tennis player. I assure you that you needn't worry about hitting the ball out or into the net because the camera will only be focused on you and will not follow the ball. What I'm mainly interested in is that you adopt professional mannerisms, and that you swing your racket with supreme self-assurance. Above all, your face must express no self-doubt. You should look as if you are hitting every ball exactly where you want to. Really get into the role, hit as hard as you like and ignore where the ball is actually going."

When a player succeeds in forgetting himself and really acts out his assumed role, remarkable changes in his game often take place; if you don't mind puns, you might even say that the changes are dramatic. As long as he is able to stay in this role he experiences qualities that he may not have known were in his repertoire.

There is an important distinction between this kind of role-playing and what is normally called positive thinking. In the latter, you are telling yourself that you are as good as Steffi Graf or

Michael Chang, while in the former you are not trying to convince yourself that you are any better than you believe you are. You are quite consciously playing a role, but in the process, you may become more aware of the range of your true capabilities.

After they have played tennis for a year or so, most people fall into a particular pattern of play from which they seldom depart. Some adopt a defensive style; they spare no effort to retrieve every ball, lob often, hit deep into the opponent's court and seldom hit the ball hard or go for a winner. The defensive player waits for his opponent to make an error and wears him down by degrees with endless patience. Some Italian clay-court players used to be the prototype for this style.

The opposite of this is the offensive style. In its extreme form the ball is hit for a winner every time. Every serve is designed to be an ace, every return of serve a clean passing shot, while volleys and overheads are all aimed to land within one or two inches of the lines.

A third common pattern is what might be called the "formal" style of play. Players in this category don't care so much where their ball goes as long as they look good stroking it. They would rather be seen using flawless form than winning the match.

In contrast, there is the competitive style of the player who will do anything to win. He runs hard and hits hard or soft, depending on what seems to bother his opponent most, exploiting his every weakness, mental and physical.

Having outlined these basic styles to a group of players, I often suggest that as an experiment they adopt the style that seems most unlike the one they have previously adopted. I also suggest that they act the role of a good player, no matter what style they have chosen. Besides being a lot of fun, this kind of role-playing can greatly increase a player's range. The defensive player learns that he can hit winners; the aggressive one finds that he can also be stylish. I have found that when players break their habitual patterns, they can greatly extend the limits of their own style and explore subdued aspects of their personality. As you gain easier access to the variety of qualities encompassed in your Self 2, you begin to realize that you can call upon any of these qualities as appropriate to the given situation on or off the tennis court.

Letting go of judgments, the art of creating images and "letting it happen" are three of the basic skills involved in the Inner Game. Before going on to the fourth and most important inner skill, that of concentration, I will devote one chapter to a discussion of *external* technique and how to master any technique without resorting to the kind of judgmental thinking and overcontrol that we have seen undermine Self 2's natural abilities.

FIVE

Discovering Technique

THE PRECEDING CHAPTERS PLACED HEAVY EMPHASIS ON THE IMPOR-
tance of quieting the thinking mind by letting go of mental self-
instructions, focusing attention and trusting the body to do what
it is capable of doing. The purpose of these chapters was to lay the
foundation for learning technique in a more natural and effective
way. Before introducing specific techniques of the various tennis
strokes, I would like to make some general comments on the relationship between technical instructions and the Self 2 learning
process.

To me it makes sense to build any system of *instruction* upon
the best possible understanding of *natural learning*, the learning
process you were born with. The less instruction interferes with
the process of learning built into your very DNA, the more effective your progress is going to be. Said another way, the less fear

and doubt are embedded in the instructional process, the easier it will be to take the natural steps of learning. One way to gain insight and trust in natural learning is to observe young children learning before they have been taught, or to observe animals in the act of teaching their young.

Once when I was walking through the San Diego Zoo, I had the chance to observe a mother hippopotamus giving her baby what looked to be its first swimming lesson. At the deep end of the pool one hippo was floating with just its nose above the surface. Soon it submerged and sank to the bottom, where it seemed to rest for about twenty seconds before pushing off with its hind legs and rising again to the surface. Then I watched a mother hippo, which had been nursing her baby in the sun, get up and begin to push it toward the pond with her snout. When the baby toppled in, it sank like a rock to the bottom and stayed there. Mother sauntered casually to the shallow end of the pool and waded in. About twenty seconds later she reached the baby and began to lift it upward with her nose, sending it toward the surface. There the young student gasped a breath and sank again. Once again the mother repeated the process, but this time moved off to the deeper end of the pool, somehow knowing that her role in the learning process was finished. The baby hippo inhaled on the surface and sank again to the bottom, but after some time, it pushed itself toward the surface with its own hind legs. Then the new skill was repeated again and again.

It seemed that the mother knew exactly how much it needed to "show," when to encourage and when encouragement was no longer needed. It knew it could trust a great deal in the instinct of the child, once it was "jump-started." Though I would not go so far as to say a topspin backhand is already imprinted within your genetic structure, I would say that the natural learning process is so encoded, and that we would do well to acknowledge and respect it. As either teacher or student we will be most ourselves and most effective only to the extent that we can be in harmony with it.

WHERE DO TECHNICAL
INSTRUCTIONS ORIGINATE?

Tennis was brought to America from Europe in the late 1800s. There were no professional tennis teachers to teach technique. The best were players who experienced certain feelings in their swings and tried to communicate those feelings to others. In the effort to understand how to use technical knowledge or theory, I believe that it is most important to recognize that, fundamentally, experience precedes technical knowledge. We may read books or articles that present technical instructions before we have ever lifted a racket, but where did these instructions come from? At some point did they not originate in someone's experience? Either by accident or by intention someone hit a ball in a certain way and it felt good and it worked. Through experimentation, refinements were made and finally settled into a repeatable stroke.

Perhaps in the interest of being able to repeat that way of hitting the ball again or to pass it on to another, the person attempts to describe that stroke in *language*. But words can only *represent* actions, ideas and experiences. Language is *not* the action, and at best can only hint at the subtlety and complexity contained in the stroke. Although the instruction thus conceived can now be stored in the part of the mind that remembers language, it must be acknowledged that remembering the instruction is not the same as remembering the stroke itself.

Of course it is very convenient to think that by giving ourselves correct instruction—"hit from low to high," for example—we will hit great topspin backhands again and again. We want to trust Self 1's conceptual process of learning technique instead of Self 2's learning from experience. Thinking that it was the obeying of an instruction that produced the good shot, ignoring the role that Self 2 plays, sets us up for disappointment when we give the same instruction yet the same good shot does not occur. Since we think the instruction was correct, the conclusion we come to is that not obeying it led to the error. Then we may get angry at ourselves, make disparaging remarks about our ability and call ourselves stupid or use a variety of ways to blame ourselves.

But maybe the error was in not trusting Self 2 enough and relying too much on Self 1 control. It is as if we would like to think of ourselves more as an obedient computer than as a human being. As a consequence, we are apt to lose access to the direct pathway to the muscle memory that carries a more complete knowledge of the desired action. In a society that has become so oriented toward language as a way of representing truth, it is very possible to lose touch with your ability to feel and with it your ability to "remember" the shots themselves. I believe this remembering is a fundamental act of trust in Self 2 without which excellence in any skill cannot be sustained.

When the verbal instruction is passed on to another person who does not have in his bank of experience the action being described in memory, it lives in the mind totally disconnected from experience. The chances are now even greater that there will be a split between memory of theory and the memory of action. (I am reminded of the lines from "The Hollow Men," by T. S. Eliot: "Between the idea / And the reality / Between the motion / And the act / Falls the Shadow.")

And as we begin to use an instruction to pass judgment on our shots instead of attending to the lessons of experience, the gap between experience and instruction is further widened. The instruction, used as a conceptual "should" or "should not," puts a shadow of fear between Self 2's intuitive knowing and the action. Many times I have seen students hitting perfectly good shots, but complaining about them because they thought they did something "wrong." By the time they have brought their stroke into conformity with their concept of the "right" way to do it, the shot has lost both power and consistency, as well as naturalness.

In short, if we let ourselves lose touch with our ability to feel our actions, by relying too heavily on instructions, we can seriously compromise our access to our natural learning processes and our potential to perform. Instead, if we hit the ball relying on the instincts of Self 2, we reinforce the simplest neural pathway to the optimal shot.

Though this discussion has been primarily theoretical up to this point, it has recently been confirmed by the United States Tennis Association Sports Science Department, as well as by almost everyone's experience, that too many verbal instructions, given either from outside or inside, interfere with one's shotmaking ability. It is also common experience that one verbal instruction given to ten different people will take on ten different meanings. Trying too hard to perform even a single instruction not well understood can introduce an awkwardness or rigidity into the swing that inhibits excellence.

In previous chapters, I made the point that a great deal of technique can be learned naturally by simply paying close attention to one's body, racket and ball while playing. The more awareness one can bring to bear on any action, the more feedback one gets from experience, and the more naturally one learns the technique that feels best and works best for any given player at any given state of development. Bottom line: there is no substitute for learning from experience. However, even though we have the ability to learn naturally, many of us have forgotten. And many of us have lost touch with feel. We may need to learn how to feel again and learn how to learn again. The saying of an old master is pertinent here: "No teacher is greater than one's own experience."

HOW TO MAKE BEST USE
OF TECHNICAL INSTRUCTIONS

So the question that remains is how one person's greater level of experience can help another person. The short answer is that a valid instruction derived from experience can help me if it *guides* me to my own experiential discovery of any given stroke possibility. From the point of view of the student, the question becomes how to listen to technical instructions and use them without falling into the Self 1 traps of judgment, doubt and fear. For the teacher or coach, the question has to be how to give instructions in such a way as to help the natural learning process of the student and not interfere with it. If insight can be gained into these questions, I believe they would be applicable to the learning of skills in many different domains.

Let's begin with a very simple yet common instruction given by many teaching professionals: "Keep the wrist firm when hitting the backhand." I would guess that this instruction originated from someone's accurate observations of the relative consistency and power of backhands hit when the wrist was firm compared to when it was loose or wobbly. As obvious as this instruction might sound at first, let's analyze it before casting it into the bronze of dogma. Can the backhand be hit with a wrist that is too loose to give control? Certainly. But can it also be hit with a wrist that is too firm? Yes, of course it can. So as helpful as this instruction might appear, you cannot use it successfully by merely "obeying" it. Instead you use the instruction to *guide your discovery* of the optimal degree of tightness of your wrist. This of course can be done by paying attention to the *feel* of your wrist during your stroke and does not necessarily have to be put into language. You will hit some shots with too loose a wrist, others perhaps with too tight a wrist, and automatically you will find what is comfortable and works best for you and settle with that. Obviously the exact degree of tightness you discovered worked for you would be very hard to put into definitive language; it is remembered by its *feel*.

This is a very different process from *obeying* the instruction. If I believe dogmatically in the "firm wrist" instruction, and if in fact my wrist has been too loose, my first shots with a firmer wrist will probably seem better to me. Then I might say to myself, "Firming my wrist is good." So on subsequent shots I remember to tell myself to firm my wrist. But on these shots my wrist was already firm, so now it is too tight. Soon the tightness is spreading all the way up my arm, to my neck, my cheeks and my lips. But I am obeying my instruction, so what went wrong? Soon somebody has to tell me to relax. But how do I relax the right amount? I go back in the other direction until I am too wobbly again.

So I believe the best use of technical knowledge is to communicate a hint toward a desired destination. The hint can be delivered verbally or demonstrated in action, but it is best seen as an approximation of a desirable *goal* to be discovered by paying attention to each stroke, and feeling one's way toward what works for that individual. If I want to give the instruction, "Hit from low to high to produce topspin," to avoid Self 1 overcontrol, I might first demonstrate with the student's racket and arm approximately what those words mean. Then I might say, "But don't try to do it, just notice if your racket is coming from high to low, is coming through level with the ball, or coming from low to high." After a few shots are hit from low to high, I might ask for more subtle awareness of the degree of low to high of successive shots. In this way the student experiences the relationship between the degree of low to high and the amount of topspin achieved, and is able to explore a range of possibilities and discover what feels best and works for himself without the constraint of thinking there is a specifically right way to do it to which he must conform.

If you asked a group of teaching professionals to write down all the important elements of hitting a forehand, most would find it easy to distinguish at least fifty, and they might have several categories for each element. Imagine the difficulty for the tennis player dealing with this complexity. No wonder self-doubt is so easy to come by! On the other hand, understanding the swing, and remembering its feel, is like remembering a single picture. The mind is capable of that, and can recognize when one element in one picture is slightly different from another. The other advantage of using awareness to "discover the technique" is that it doesn't tend to evoke the overcontrolling and judgmental aspects of Self 1, which wants to rely on formula rather than feel.

The remainder of this chapter will offer a few technical instructions that you can use to help you discover effective technique for each of the major strokes in tennis. The effort is not to give all the instructions that you might eventually need, but to give enough of a sample that you can better understand how to use *any* technical instructions from any source as a means toward your discovery of *your* optimal stroke production.

Before beginning, let me simplify the external requirements of tennis. The player has only two requirements for success: hit each ball over the net and into the court. The sole aim of stroke technique is to fulfill these two requirements with consistency and enough pace and accuracy to provide maximum difficulty for one's opponent. Keeping it simple, let's look at a few of the dynamics for hitting forehand and backhand ground strokes over the net and into the court. One thing we will see is that the officially approved techniques for doing this have changed considerably over the years. That which was dogmatically true is no longer so true.

GROUND STROKES

Grips

If you were to ask ten tennis players why they hold their racket with one grip when hitting the forehand, and a different grip when hitting the backhand, most would probably answer that they read it in a book or magazine, or were taught it by their pro. Even though what they were told might be "correct," if they have little *experiential* understanding of grips or why you change them, it is unlikely that they will really discover the best grips for their game.

A great deal of information about grips is readily available. One reason players have learned to change grips is to provide the strongest bond between racket and hand on each shot. But because every hand is slightly different, the exact positioning of your grip should be adjusted according to what is comfortable for your hand, while allowing the desired support and racket angle.

The same goes for how tightly you should grip the racket.

Just try to describe this in language! My best effort at this was borrowed from a fencing instruction given to Cyrano de Bergerac: "Hold the foil as a bird, not so loosely that it can fly away, but not so tightly that you squeeze the life out of it." It is a nice metaphor. But in reality, the only way to find the right degree of pressure to apply to the grip is by experiencing it in action and discovering what feels comfortable and what works.

If you have been following the evolution of "approved" grips in the last few years, you will have noticed the dominance of the universally approved Eastern forehand grip ("shake hands" grip with the V formed by the thumb and forefinger on the top panel of the racket). Although this is still the grip approved in United States Tennis Association publications, it has been abandoned by many tournament players in favor of the "semi-Western grip" (approximately a quarter turn to the right of the Eastern grip— for right-handed players). How did these players come to use this grip? And why are they sticking with it? Could it be that they *discovered* it, and that their experience has continued to validate its use? They broke with dogma, not because the dogma was wrong, but because they found something that worked better for them.

Footwork

Footwork is clearly one of the critical variables for the successful execution of any shot in tennis. It provides the foundation that supports the body's movement as it swings to hit the ball. Much has been written about this subject and it is all too easy to get the feet tangled or feel awkward in the process of "obeying" a myriad of footwork instructions. We will take another approach.

The footwork technique most commonly taught by teaching professionals on the backhand has remained relatively unchanged over the past twenty years. Right-handed players are typically instructed to "hit the ball with your feet moving forward toward the ball at an approximately 45-degree angle with your feet comfortably separated." It is commonly explained that "one tends to lose balance if the feet are too close together," and that "your weight should transfer from the back foot toward the front foot as you move to strike the ball."

Assuming that these two instructions can be useful guides to learning footwork technique, how can they best be used? First, resist the temptation to immediately obey them. The first step is to closely observe your own footwork especially as it relates to one of the variables in the instruction, say, weight *transfer*. Without making any conscious changes in your weight shift, simply observe how the transfer is occurring now. As you continue your observation, chances are your weight will automatically begin to make some changes, that is if any change is needed. You can let Self 2 experiment until it finds what feels best and works best for you.

The same approach can be used with discovering the proper angle. Knowing what 45 degrees might look like, you can simply observe the angle with which your front foot steps toward the ball. If during your initial observations you observe your foot moving significantly less or more than the desired angle, don't force it. Just allow Self 2 to approximate the desired angle until it feels comfortable. You are asking; it is executing. Be prepared for the fact that sometimes Self 2 may find that what works best for it is not in conformity with the instruction. Such might well be the case with the footwork on the forehand side.

In contrast to the backhand, what has been accepted as correct footwork on the forehand has changed dramatically over the past twenty years. When the first edition of this book was published, it was commonly taught that the footwork on the forehand should be close to the same as on the backhand, except with the other foot moving forward toward the ball at approximately a 45-degree angle. That was certainly the way I was taught when I first learned the game over fifty years ago. In fact, when I learned, the "correct" footwork steps were painted on a black rubber mat. To learn the prescribed footwork on the running forehand, I was trained to place my feet in the printed steps over and over again until I could do it without looking. Then, when taking my lesson, failure to reproduce that exact footwork was a cue to the instructor to give corrective instructions.

However, now there are two alternative and commonly approved footworks recommended. One way, called the "open stance forehand," was discovered and propagated by clay-court players who began hitting with weight established on their right, or back foot, instead of transferring weight to the front foot. Instead of stepping into the ball with the left foot, they would step horizontally, parallel to the baseline, with their right foot assuming an almost 180-degree stance. They would turn their shoulders, rotate their hips and unwind like a corkscrew to hit the ball. Easier to observe than to describe, the open stance forehand proved very effective on clay courts and ultimately was adapted by many professionals playing on hard courts or grass as well. It had the advantage of making it easier to produce topspin and also to return to the center of the court faster than when hitting off of one's left foot. This evolution is especially interesting to me, as I remember the countless times I was scolded for hitting the forehand in this way, before it had become "approved."

To learn the footwork for this "open stance" forehand along with the other elements of the swing that go with it would be a daunting task if you had to break it into its component parts, learn them by means of instructions and then put them all together. However, it might not be so difficult to learn if you observed someone who did the stroke well, let yourself "play around with it," before putting your attention to the details of the swing. During this experiment it would be important to be totally nonjudgmental, even unconcerned about your results, until you got a feel for the swing as a whole. Not until then would you focus your attention on the specifics and allow them to refine themselves. When you felt ready, you might choose to focus attention on how much your hips were rotating, observe your shoulder turn, the action of your arm, etc. You would observe each of these in turn just as you did the weight distribution of your feet on the backhand, without any conscious effort to make them conform to a certain pattern, but allowing yourself to discover the *feel* that is comfortable for your body and personality and produces effective results.

If you learned how to hit the open stance forehand, that does not mean that you have to use it on every shot or that it is even the correct way to hit the forehand. The other accepted technique for hitting the forehand, called the semi-open stance, is done by forming a 90- to 100-degree angle between your two feet and the baseline. Obviously this is a compromise between the traditional footwork and the open stance forehand and shares some of the advantages of each. If you so choose, you can master all three forehands, and use each when it seems appropriate. The important thing is that the choice is kept in your court, and that instead of trying to fit yourself or your stroke into a preconceived model, you fit the models to you and use them only to help you discover and develop the skills you desire. To do otherwise is to diminish your potential as a player, and as a learner.

When you understand how simple attention can be used to learn any technical aspect of the game, with or without the aid of a technical instruction as a guide, it is quite an easy matter to discover the important places to focus your attention, and then use the same simple process of discovering from experience. A few critical focal points for the ground strokes are summarized below. You could take any instruction from any tennis magazine or book and add to the list.

A partial ground stroke checklist

1. *Backswing*   Exactly where is the head of your racket at the back of your swing? Where is the ball when you initiate your backswing? What happens with the face of the racket during the backswing?

2. *Impact*   Can you feel where the ball is meeting the racket at impact? How is your weight distributed? What is the

angle of racket face at impact? How long can you feel the ball on the face of the racket? To what extent can you feel the kind and amount of spin being imparted to the ball? How solid does the shot feel or how much vibration is sent up your arm at impact? How far in front of or behind you is the ball at impact?

3. *Follow-through* Where does your racket finish? In what direction? What has happened to the face of the racket since impact? Is there any hesitancy or resistance experienced during the follow-through?

4. *Footwork* How is your weight distributed during preparation and at impact? What happens to your balance during the shot? How many steps did you take to get to the ball? What size are the steps? What kinds of sounds do your feet make on the court as you move? When the ball approaches you, do you retreat, advance or hold your ground? From how solid a base are you hitting the ball?

THE SERVE

Compared with the other strokes of tennis, the serve is the most complicated. Both arms are involved in the stroke, and your hitting arm is making simultaneous movements of shoulder, elbow and wrist. The movements of the serve are much too complicated for Self 1 to master by memorizing instructions for each element of the stroke. But it is not so difficult if you let Self 2 do the learning by focusing attention on the different elements of the stroke as well as the stroke as a whole.

Some Places to Focus Attention on the Serve

In general, there are some specific places where it can help to focus your attention for practicing your serve. Remember the fundamental goal is still the same, over the net and into the court with power, accuracy and consistency. Here are just a few variables to consider.

THE TOSS

- How high is it?
- How far does it drop, if at all, before contact with your racket?
- How much forward or behind, right or left of the toe of your front foot?

BALANCE

- Is there any time during the serve when you feel off balance?
- What is the direction of your momentum at follow-through?
- How is your weight distributed during the serve?

RHYTHM

- Observe the rhythm of your serve. Count the cadence of the rhythm you feel by saying, "da . . . da . . . da," one "da" at the moment you start the serve, one at hit, as you bring the racket up, and one at contact. Feel and listen to the rhythm until you find what feels best and works best for you.

RACKET POSITION AND WRIST SNAP

- Where is your racket at the moment before moving forward toward the ball?
- Is your racket coming around the right side of the ball or the left? Hitting it flat, or coming from left to right? To what extent?
- To what extent is your wrist snapping at impact?
- At what point in the swing does it begin to release?

Power

Because power is so sought after on the serve, it is not unusual for players to "try too hard" to produce it, and in the process to over-tighten the muscles of wrist and arm. Ironically, the over-tightening of these muscles has the opposite effect on power. It reduces power, by making it more difficult for the wrist and elbow to release freely. So again, the important point is to *observe* the tightness of your muscles so that you can experientially find the degree of tension that provides the best results.

Your teaching pro can be helpful in pointing out the best focus of attention for your particular serve at its current state of development. As long as you take his guidance as an opportunity to explore your own experience, you really cannot help but learn in a natural and effective manner.

Besides the fact that we all have to learn as individuals, it is also obvious that there is no one best way to serve for everyone. If there were, why do so many of the best servers in tennis today serve so differently? Each may have learned things from others, but each of them evolved over time a way of serving that suited his own body, skill level, personality traits—in short, himself. And their process is still evolving. And in spite of all the credit they might give to different players or coaches for helping them find their serves, their primary development was directed from within themselves by that simple process of what feels good and what works for each individual.

As with many of the other strokes in tennis, the orthodox approach to the serve is under challenge by pros who seem to be breaking out of its mold. When I learned to serve some fifty years ago, my coach, John Gardiner, one of the best in the field, taught the approved method of the time. To get the arms moving in the correct direction and rhythm, we chanted the mantra, "down together, up together, hit." What this meant was that both the tossing and the hitting arm were brought down at the same time. Then as the tossing arm was raised to toss the ball, the hitting arm was also raised and dropped down the back, poised for the moment of hit—much like a football quarterback cocks his arm in preparation to throw a forward pass. Then depending on how high the ball was tossed, the hitting arm would surge forward to strike the ball so that it would be fully extended at impact, and then follow through past the feet. Basic tennis gospel for fifty years.

Then just today, in the midst of writing this section on serving, I read an article in this month's *Tennis* magazine that pointed out that the best servers in the game today, including Steffi Graf, Todd Martin, Pete Sampras, Mark Philippoussis and Goran Ivanisevic, do not in fact follow this down-together-up-together motion. So from the point of view of the "right way" to serve, all these great players are doing it "wrong."

The article was entitled "Stagger Your Arms for Serving" and the author recommended that when the tossing arm is fully extended for the toss, the hitting arm should still be pointing down toward the court. To learn to serve like these pros, the player is instructed thusly: "*As the tossing arm rises, drop the hitting arm back and down,*" followed by this explanation:

> The old "up together" technique, which may seem more rhythmic, actually works against creating power for some players, because it forces the hitting arm to pause at the top of the backswing, destroying the build-up of momentum to that point.

The pictures of these pros serving makes it obvious that they are doing something very differently. The instruction continues:

> Most important of all, note how each of these players has his or her hitting arm in the "palm-down" position: i.e., the hitting-hand palm is facing the ground at the moment the ball is released. . . . This is necessary to achieve the "lasso effect" of a good serve, in which the racquet is then quickly raised above the head and circled down around the back before snapping up to strike the ball.

I cite this instruction for two reasons: first, to show that gospels change and they are changed by people who had the courage to experiment outside the boundaries of the existing doctrine and trust in their own learning process. The second reason is to suggest that the prescribed way of making a change itself needs to change. When I read the above instruction for the so-called staggered arm timing, my mind is beset with several doubts. Do I even understand what is meant by such terms as "lasso effect" or "hitting-hand palm is facing the ground"? The next doubt that knocks at my door is, even if I did understand the instructions, could I follow them? Then, I wonder if I am going to be able to get rid of my "old way" of serving that I've practiced diligently for years. And finally, just because this way of serving works for professionals at their level, does that mean it is best for me?

So how can you benefit from such an article that may in fact be pointing out a valid new discovery about the serve? First you might want to get clear on *why* you might want to experiment with making a change in the first place. It may not be sufficient reason that some top pros serve differently now or that this way of serving is coming into fashion. On the other hand, you may feel that if there is a way for you to increase power on your serve it would be worth the effort of *experimentation* for you. This first step of knowing what results *you* want is critical to maintaining control of the learning process where it belongs—with you.

After reading an article or watching some people serve with the new method, don't jump to the conclusion that this new way is necessarily "right" for you. Just let yourself (Self 2) observe whatever it finds interesting, and ignore comments from Self 1, which will want to be making up little formulas for you to follow. As you observe, certain things will "stand out" or come to the foreground of your attention spontaneously. Allow Self 2 to focus on elements that in its intelligence it might be ready to experiment with.

HOW TO WATCH THE PROS

When I was a child, I used to play touch football, and I noticed that I played quite a lot better when I'd just come home after my Dad had taken me to see the San Francisco 49ers play. I hadn't studied the passing technique of Frankie Albert. But I had picked up something, and it made a difference when I played. I think most people have experienced something very similar to this.

Although it is obvious that we can learn a great deal by watching better players play tennis, we have to learn how to watch. The best method is to simply watch without assuming that how the pro swings is how you should be swinging. In many cases, for a beginner to try to swing like a pro would be like asking a baby to walk before it has crawled. To formulate technique while watching the pro or by trying to imitate too closely can be detrimental to your natural learning process.

Instead allow yourself to focus on whatever most interests you about the movements of the pro you are watching. Self 2 will automatically pick up elements of the stroke that are useful to it and discard what is not useful. With each new swing, observe how it feels and how it works. Allow the natural learning process to lead you toward your best stroke. Do not force yourself to make the change. Just allow Self 2 to "play around" while it searches for new stroke possibilities. In doing so it will use what it can of the "hints" picked up in observation of the pro.

Based on my experience and the experience of those I have worked with, Self 2 has very good instincts about when it is time to work on any particular element of your stroke. In learning how to learn by watching pros play, you may want to alternate between external observation and experimentation on the court, until you have confidence that you can access the particular stroke technique you are working on.

With the Inner Game approach, the final authority stays inside during the alternation between external observation (or remembrance of an external instruction) and total focus of awareness on your own movements. But there is no judgment necessary in the process. You see differences between what you are doing and the external model, but simply notice them and continue to observe, feel your own movements and check the results. The prevailing learning mind-set is a freedom to search for the feel that works for you.

In summary, I believe someone who has discovered his or her best stroke *can* help you discover your best stroke. Knowledge of technique learned by one person can give another an advantage in discovering what technique works best. But it is dangerous to make that person's stroke or any stroke description into your standard for right and wrong. Self 1 easily gets enamored of formulas that tell it where the racket should be and when. It likes the feeling of control it gets from doing it by the book. But Self 2 likes the feeling of flow—of the whole stroke as one thing. The Inner Game is an encouragement to keep in touch with the Self 2 learning process you were born with while avoiding getting caught up in trying too hard to make your strokes conform to an outside model. Use outside models in your learning, but don't let them use you. Natural learning is and always will be from the inside out, not vice versa. *You* are the learner and it is your individual, internal learning process that ultimately governs your learning.

What I like about this approach is that I do not have the feeling that I am fitting myself or my students into an external model that may be in fashion for the moment, but that I am using any external model to further help me take a step in the natural evolution toward *my* very best strokes. After an Inner Game tennis lesson, a golf professional put it this way: "What I consider to be the right technique for my swing is ever-changing day by day. My model is always being destroyed and rebuilt as I learn more and more. My technique is always evolving." Self 2's nature is to evolve every chance it gets. As your technique evolves, you will start to become better at learning technique and be able to make big changes in a short period of time. As you discover Self 2's learning capabilities, not only will your tennis strokes improve, but you will have increased your capacity to learn anything.

Opposite is a table that can give you an idea of how to take instructions on any strokes from a pro, a tennis magazine or book, and alter them into an awareness instruction that will facilitate the discovery of your own optimal technique. These observations should be made over the course of as many shots as it takes until Self 2 has had the chance to experiment and has settled on its preferred stroke. If you have a teacher, let him or her teach, but keep Self 2 in control, because it really is your greatest resource.

STROKE	TECHNICAL INSTRUCTION	AWARENESS INSTRUCTION
GROUND STROKES	Follow through at shoulder level.	Notice the level of your follow-through relative to your shoulder.
	Take your racket back early.	Observe where your racket is when the ball bounces.
	Get down to the ball.	Feel the extent of knee bend on the next ten shots.
	Take the racket back below the level of the ball to produce topspin.	Notice the level of your racket in relation to the ball at impact. Feel the contact and notice the amount of topspin produced.
	Hit the ball in the center of the racket.	Sense (not with your eyes) where the ball makes contact with the racket face.
	Plant your back foot when setting up for your ground stroke.	Notice what percent of your weight is on your back foot as you prepare to hit your ground strokes
VOLLEY	Hit the ball in front of you.	Notice where you are making contact with the ball.
	Volley the ball deep into the opponent's court.	Notice where your volleys are landing in relation to the baseline.
	Don't take a backswing. Punch the ball.	How far back are you taking your racket? What is the minimum amount possible? What amount of backswing provides the best opportunity to punch the ball?

STROKE	TECHNICAL INSTRUCTION	AWARENESS INSTRUCTION
	Whenever possible, strike the ball before it drops below the level of the net.	Focus on the *space* between the ball and the top of the net. Notice the differing amounts.
SERVE	Hit the ball with your arm fully extended.	Notice the degree of bend in your elbow at the moment of impact with the ball.
	Toss the ball as high as the extended arm and racket, and about six inches in front of your lead foot.	Observe the height of your toss. Let the ball drop and notice where it lands in relation to your lead foot.

SIX

Changing Habits

THE PREVIOUS CHAPTER MAY HAVE GIVEN YOU SOME IDEAS ABOUT changes you would like to make in your tennis strokes. The aim of this chapter is to summarize the Inner Game method of how to effect such changes so that they become a spontaneous part of your behavior. Tips are a dime a dozen, and there are good ones and bad ones. But what is more difficult to come by is a workable way to apply tips, to replace one pattern of behavior with a new one. It is in the process of changing habits that most players experience the greatest difficulty. When one learns *how* to change a habit, it is a relatively simple matter to learn *which* ones to change. Once you learn *how* to learn, you have only to discover *what* is worth learning.

Summarized below is what could be called a new way of learning. Actually, it is not new at all; it is the oldest and most natural way of learning—simply a method of forgetting the unnatural ways of learning that we have accumulated. Why is it so easy for a child to pick up a foreign language? Primarily because he hasn't learned how to interfere with his own natural, untaught learning process. The Inner Game way of learning is a return toward this childlike way.

By the word "learning" I do not mean the collection of information, but the realization of something which actually changes one's behavior—either external behavior, such as a tennis stroke, or internal behavior, such as a pattern of thought. We all develop characteristic patterns of acting and thinking, and each such pattern exists because it serves a function. The time for change comes when we realize that the same function could be served in a better way. Take the habit of rolling one's racket over after hitting a forehand. This behavior is an attempt to keep the ball from going out, and it exists to produce the desired result. But when the player realizes that by the proper use of topspin the ball can be kept in the court without the risks of error involved in a roll-over follow-through, then the old habit is ready to be dropped.

It is much more difficult to break a habit when there is no adequate replacement for it. This difficulty often exists when we become moralistic about our tennis game. If a player reads in a book that it is wrong to roll his racket over, but is not offered a better way to keep the ball in the court, it will take a great deal of willpower to keep his racket flat when he's worried about the ball flying out of the court. As soon as this player gets into a game, you can be sure that he will revert to the stroke that gave some sense of security that his ball would not sail out.

It is not helpful to condemn our present behavior patterns—in this case our present imperfect strokes—as "bad"; it *is* helpful to see what function these habits are serving, so that if we learn a better way to achieve the same end, we can do so. We never repeat any behavior which isn't serving some function or purpose. It is difficult to become aware of the function of any pattern of behavior while we are in the process of blaming ourselves for having a "bad habit." But when we stop trying to suppress or correct the habit, we can see the function it serves, and then an alternative pattern of behavior, which serves the same function better, emerges quite effortlessly.

THE GROOVE THEORY OF HABITS

One hears a lot of talk about grooving one's strokes in tennis. The theory is a simple one: every time you swing your racket in a certain way, you increase the probabilities that you will swing that way again. In this way patterns, called grooves, build up which have a predisposition to repeat themselves. Golfers use the same term. It is as if the nervous system were like a record disk. Every time an action is performed, a slight impression is made in the microscopic cells of the brain, just as a leaf blowing over a fine-grained beach of sand will leave its faint trace. When the same action is repeated, the groove is made slightly deeper. After many similar actions there is a more recognizable groove into which the needle of behavior seems to fall automatically. Then the behavior can be termed grooved.

Because these patterns are serving a function, the behavior is reinforced or rewarded and tends to continue. The deeper the groove in the nervous system, the harder it seems to be to break the habit. We have all had the experience of deciding that we will not hit a tennis ball a certain way again. For example, it would seem to be a simple matter to keep your eye on the ball once you understand the obvious benefits of doing so. But time and again we take our eye off it. Often, in fact, the harder we try to break a habit, the harder it becomes to do.

If you watch a player trying to correct the habit of rolling his racket over, he will usually be seen gritting his teeth and exerting all his willpower to get out of his old groove. Watch his racket. After it hits the ball it will begin to turn over, following the old pattern; then his muscles will tighten and force it to return to the flat position. You can see in the resulting waver exactly where the old habit was halted and the new willpower took over. Usually the battle is won, if at all, only after a great deal of struggle and frustration over the course of some time.

It is a painful process to fight one's way out of deep mental grooves. It's like digging yourself out of a trench. But there is a natural and more childlike method. A child doesn't dig his way out of his old grooves; he simply starts new ones! The groove may be there, but you're not in it unless you put yourself there. If you think you are controlled by a bad habit, then you will feel you have to try to break it. A child doesn't have to break the habit of crawling, because he doesn't think he has a habit. He simply leaves it as he finds walking an easier way to get around.

Habits are statements about the past, and the past is gone. There may be a deep groove in the nervous system which will take your forehand on the roll-over trip if you choose to step into that trench; on the other hand, your muscles are as capable as they ever were of swinging your racket through flat. There is no need to strain all the muscles in the arm to keep the racket flat; in fact, it requires fewer muscles to keep it flat than it does to roll it over. Fighting the fantasy of old habits is what causes the conscientious tennis player to strain and tighten unnecessarily.

In short, there is no need to fight old habits. Start new ones. It is the resisting of an old habit that puts you in that trench. Starting a new pattern is easy when done with childlike disregard for imagined difficulties. You can prove this to yourself by your own experience.

MAKING A CHANGE IN STROKE, STEP BY STEP

Here is a simple summary of the traditional way we have been taught to learn, contrasted with the Inner Game of learning. Experiment with this method and you will discover a workable way to make any desired change in your game.

Step 1: Nonjudgmental Observation

Where do you want to start? What part of your game needs attention? It is not always the stroke that you judge as worst which is the most ready for change. It is good to pick the stroke you most *want* to change. Let the stroke tell you if it wants to change. When you want to change what is ready to change, then the process flows.

For example, let's assume it is your serve that you decide to focus your attention on. The first step is to forget all the ideas you may have in your mind about what is wrong with it as it is. Erase all your previous ideas and begin serving without exercising any conscious control over your stroke. Observe your serve freshly, as it is *now*. Let it fall into its own groove for better or worse. Begin to be interested in it and experience it as fully as you can. Notice how you stand and distribute your weight before beginning your motion. Check your grip and the initial position of your racket. Remember, make no corrections; simply observe without interfering.

Next, get in touch with the rhythm of your serving motion. Feel the path of your racket as it describes its swing. Then serve several balls and watch only your wrist motion. Is your wrist limber or tight? Does it have a full snap or something less? Merely watch. Also observe your toss during several serves. Experience your tossing motion. Does the ball go to the same spot each time? Where is that spot? Finally, become aware of your follow-through. Before long you will feel that you know your serve very well as it is presently grooved. You may also be aware of the results of your motion—that is, the number of balls hit into the net, the speed and accuracy of those that reach the far court. Awareness of what *is*, without judgment, is relaxing, and is the best precondition for change.

It is not unlikely that during this observation period some changes have already begun to take place unintentionally. If so, let the process continue. There's nothing wrong with making unconscious changes; you avoid the complication of thinking that *you* made the change, and thus of the need to remind yourself how to do it.

After you have watched and felt your serve for five minutes or so, you may have a strong idea about the particular element of the stroke that needs attention. Ask your serve how it would like to be different. Maybe it wants a more fluid rhythm; maybe it wants more power, or a greater amount of spin. If 90 percent of the balls are going into the net, it's probably quite obvious what needs to change. In any case, let yourself feel the change most desired, then observe a few more serves.

Step 2: Picture the Desired Outcome

Let's assume that what is desired in your serve is more power. The next step is to picture your serve with more power. One way to do this might be to watch the motion of someone who gets a lot of power in his serve. Don't overanalyze; simply absorb what you see and try to feel what he feels. Listen to the sound of the ball after it hits the racket and watch the results. Then take some time to imagine yourself hitting the ball with power, using the stroke which is natural to you. In your mind's eye, picture yourself serving, filling in as much visual and tactile detail as you can. Hear the sound at impact and see the ball speed toward the service court.

Step 3: Trust Self 2

Begin serving again, but with no conscious effort to control your stroke. In particular, resist any temptation to try to hit the ball harder. Simply let your serve begin to serve itself. Having asked for more power, just let it happen. This isn't magic, so give your body a chance to explore the possibilities. But no matter what the results, keep Self 1 out of it. If increased power does not come immediately, don't force it. Trust the process, and let it happen.

If after a short while the serve does not seem to be moving in the direction of increased power, you may want to return to Step 1. Ask yourself what is inhibiting speed. If you don't come up with an answer, you might ask a pro to take a look. Let's say the pro observes that you are not getting a maximum wrist snap at the top of your swing. He may observe that one reason is that you are holding your racket too tightly to allow for flexibility. The habit of holding the racket tightly and swinging with a stiff wrist usually comes from a conscious attempt to hit the ball hard.

Experience how it *feels* to hold your racket with different degrees of firmness. Allow your wrist to show you what it feels like to move in a full, flexible arc. Don't assume you know just because you've been told; let yourself *feel* the wrist motion intimately. If you are in any doubt, ask the pro to show you the motion, not tell you about it. Then, in your mind's eye imagine your serving motion, this time seeing distinctly your wrist moving from a fully cocked position, reaching up to the sky, then snapping down until it points to the court on the follow-through. After you have fixed the image of your new wrist motion, serve again. Remember that if you *try* to snap your wrist, it will probably overtighten, so just let it go. Let it be flexible; allow it to snap in an ever-increasing arc as much as it wants to. Encourage it, but don't force it. Not trying does not mean being limp. Discover for yourself what it *does* mean.

Step 4: Nonjudgmental Observation of Change and Results

As you are letting your serve serve itself, your job is simply to observe. Watch the process without exercising control over it. If you feel you want to help, don't. The more you can bring yourself to put trust in the natural process that is at work, the less you will tend to fall into the usual interfering patterns of trying too hard, judging and thinking—and the frustration that inevitably follows.

During this process it is still important to have a certain lack of concern for where the ball is going. As you allow one element of a stroke to change, others will be affected. As you increase your wrist snap, you will alter your rhythm and timing. Initially this may result in inconsistency, but if you continue with the process, simply allowing the serve to serve itself while you remain attentive and patient, the other elements of the serve will make the needed adjustments.

Since power is a function of more than the wrist, after your snap is grooved you may want to let your attention shift to your toss, your balance or some other element. Observe these, and allow changes to occur. Serve until you have reason to believe that a groove has been established. To test if the groove is there, serve a few balls with all your attention solely on the ball. Be engrossed in the seams of the ball as you throw the ball into the air so that you are sure that your mind is not telling your body what to do. If the serve is serving itself in the new manner, a groove has automatically been started.

THE USUAL WAY OF LEARNING

STEP 1   Criticize or Judge Past Behavior

Examples: I'm hitting my forehand rotten again today. . . . Dammit, why do I keep missing those easy setups? . . . I'm not doing anything the coach told me to do in my last lesson. You were great rallying, now you're playing worse than your grand-mother . . . $%#¢*#¢$!
(The above is usually delivered in a punitive, belittling tone.)

STEP 2   Tell Yourself to Change, Instructing with
          Word Commands Repeatedly

Examples: Keep your racket low, keep your racket low, keep your racket low. Hit the ball in front of you, in front, in front . . . No, dammit, further! Don't flick your wrist, keep it stiff. . . . You stupid bum, you did it again . . . Toss the ball good and high this time, then reach up, remember to snap your wrist, and don't change grips in midserve. Hit this one into the crosscourt corner.

STEP 3   Try Hard; Make Yourself Do It Right

In this step, Self 1, having told Self 2 what to do, tries to control the action. Unnecessary body and facial muscles are used. There is a tightness which prevents maximum fluidity of stroke and precision of movement. Self 2 is not trusted.

STEP 4   Critical Judgment About Results Leading
          to a Self 1 Vicious Cycle

When one has tried hard to perform an action "right," it is difficult not to become either frustrated at failure or anxious about success. Both emotions are distracting to one's focus, and prevent full experiencing of what happens. Negative judgment of the results of one's efforts tends to make one *try* even harder; positive evaluation tends to make one *try* to force oneself into the same pattern on the next shot. Both positive and negative thinking inhibit spontaneity.

THE INNER GAME WAY OF LEARNING

STEP 1   Observe Existing Behavior Nonjudgmentally

Examples: The last three of my backhands landed long, by about two feet. My racket seems to be hesitating, instead of following through all the way. Maybe I should observe the level of my backswing . . . It's well above my waist . . . There, that shot got hit with more pace, yet it stayed in.

(The above is delivered in an interested, somewhat detached tone.)

STEP 2   Picture Desired Outcome

No commands are used. Self 2 is asked to perform in the desired way to achieve the desired results. Self 2 is shown by use of visual image and felt action any element of stroke desired. If you wish the ball to go to the crosscourt corner, you simply imagine the necessary path of the ball to the target. Do not try to correct for past errors.

STEP 3   Let It Happen! Trust Self 2

Having requested your body to perform a certain action, give it the freedom to do it. The body is trusted, without the conscious control of mind. The serve seems to serve itself. *Effort* is initiated by Self 2, but there is no trying by Self 1. Letting it happen doesn't mean going limp; it means letting Self 2 use only the muscles necessary for the job. Nothing is forced. Continue the process. Be willing to allow Self 2 to make changes within changes, until a natural groove is formed.

STEP 4   Nonjudgmental, Calm Observation of the Results
            Leading to Continuing Observation and Learning

Though the player knows his goal, he is not emotionally involved in achieving it and is therefore able to watch the results calmly and experience the process. By so doing, concentration is best achieved, as is learning at its highest rate of speed; making new changes is only necessary when results do not conform to the image given. Otherwise only continuing observation of the behavior undergoing change is necessary. Watch it change; don't do the changing.

The process is an incredibly simple one. The important thing is to experience it. Don't intellectualize it. See what it feels like to ask yourself to do something and let it happen without any conscious trying. For most people it is a surprising experience, and the results speak for themselves.

This method of learning can be practiced in most endeavors on or off the court. The more you let yourself perform free of control on the tennis court, the more confidence you tend to gain in the beautiful mechanism that is the human body. The more you trust it, the more capable it seems to become.

WATCH OUT FOR THE RETURN OF SELF 1

But there is one pitfall I should mention. I have noticed that after being thrilled by the improvements they are able to make in their tennis game by letting it happen, students often revert the next day to trying as hard as usual. What is surprising is that though they are playing much worse tennis, they don't seem to mind. At first this puzzled me. Why would one go back to letting Self 1 control the show if the results were so clearly less effective? I had to search myself for the answer. I realized that there was a distinctly different kind of satisfaction gained in the two methods of hitting the ball. When you try hard to hit the ball correctly, and it goes well, you get a certain kind of ego satisfaction. You feel that *you* are in control, that you are master of the situation. But when you simply allow the serve to serve itself, it doesn't seem as if you deserve the credit. It doesn't feel as if it were you who hit the ball. You tend to feel good about the ability of your body, and possibly even amazed by the results, but the credit and sense of personal accomplishment are replaced by another kind of satisfaction. If a person is out on the court mainly to satisfy the desires and doubts of ego, it is likely that in spite of the lesser results, he will choose to let Self 1 play the major role.

GIVE SELF 2 THE CREDIT

When a player experiences what it means to "let go" and allows Self 2 to play the game, not only do his shots tend to gain accuracy and power, but he feels an exhilarating sense of relaxation even during rapid movements. In an attempt to repeat this quality of performance, the player often allows Self 1 to creep back on the scene with a remark such as, "Now I've got the secret to this game; all I have to do is make myself relax." But of course the instant I *try* to make myself relax, true relaxation vanishes, and in its place is a strange phenomenon called "trying to relax." Relaxation happens only when *allowed*, not as a result of "trying" or "making."

Self 1 should not be expected to give up its control all at once; it begins to find its proper role only as one progresses in the art of relaxed concentration.

SEVEN

Concentration:
Learning to Focus

Up to this point we have been discussing the art of letting go of Self 1 control and letting Self 2 play the game spontaneously. The primary emphasis has been on giving practical examples of the value of letting go of self-judging, thinking too much, trying too hard—all forms of overcontrol. But even if the reader is wholly convinced of the value of thus quieting Self 1, it may not be found to come easily. My experience over the years is that the best way to quiet the mind is not by telling it to shut up, or by arguing with it, or criticizing it for criticizing you. Fighting the mind does not work. *What works best is learning to focus it.* Learning to focus is the subject of this chapter and to whatever extent we learn this primary art, it can benefit us in most anything we do.

Strangely, even when one has experienced the practical benefit of a still mind, we continue to find it an elusive state. In spite of the fact that I deliver my most effective performance when I permit the spontaneous Self 2 to be in control, there is still a recurring impulse to think about how I did it, make a formula out of it and thus to bring it into Self 1's domain where it can feel in control. Sometimes I recognize this impulse as the persistent Self 1 wanting to gain credit, to be something it really isn't, and in the process spawning an endless flow of distracting thoughts that distort both perception and response.

There was a time at the beginning of my exploration of the Inner Game that I found myself able to let go of almost all conscious effort on my serve and as a result the serve just seemed to serve itself with rare consistency and power. For a period of about two weeks 90 percent of my first serves went in; I didn't serve a single double fault. Then one day my roommate, another professional, challenged me to a match. I accepted, saying half jokingly, "But you better watch out, I've found the secret to the serve." The next day we played and I served two double faults the first game! The moment I *tried* to apply some "secret," Self 1 was back in the picture again, this time under the subtle guise of "trying to let go." Self 1 wanted to show off to my roommate; it wanted the credit. Even though I soon realized what had happened, the magic of the spontaneous, effortless serving didn't return in its same pure form for some time.

In short, the problem of letting go of Self 1 and its interfering activities is not easy. A clear understanding of the problem can help, but practical demonstrations help more and practicing the process of letting go helps still more. Nevertheless, I do not believe that ultimately the mind can be controlled by the mere act of letting go—that is, by a simply passive process. To still the mind one must learn to put it somewhere. It cannot just be let go; it must be focused. If peak performance is a function of a still mind, then we are led to the question of where and how to focus it.

As one achieves focus, the mind quiets. As the mind is kept in the present, it becomes calm. Focus means keeping the mind now and here. Relaxed concentration is the supreme art because no art can be achieved without it, while with it, much can be achieved. One cannot reach the limit of one's potential in tennis or any endeavor without learning it; what is even more compelling is that tennis can be a marvelous medium through which skill in focus of mind can be developed. By learning to focus while playing tennis, one develops a skill that can heighten performance in every other aspect of life.

To learn this art, practice is needed. And there is never a time or situation that you cannot practice, save perhaps sleep. In tennis the most convenient and practical object of focus is the ball itself. Probably the most often repeated dictum in tennis is "Watch the ball," yet few players see it well. The instruction is an appeal for the player to simply "pay attention." It *does not* mean to think about the ball, how easy or difficult this shot is to make, how I should swing my racket at it, or what Tom, Dick or Harry will think if I make the shot or miss it. The focused mind only picks up on those aspects of a situation that are needed to accomplish the task at hand. It is not distracted by other thoughts or external events, it is totally engrossed in whatever is relevant in the here and now.

WATCHING THE BALL

Watching the ball means to focus your attention on the sight of it. I have found that the most effective way to deepen concentration through sight is to focus on something subtle, not easily perceived. It's easy to see the ball, but not so easy to notice the exact pattern made by its seams as it spins. The practice of watching the seams produces interesting results. After a short time the player discovers that he is seeing the ball much better than when he was just "watching" it. When looking for the pattern made by the seams one naturally watches the ball all the way to one's racket and begins to focus his attention on it earlier than before. The ball should be watched from the time it leaves the opponent's racket to the time it hits yours. (Sometimes the ball even begins to appear bigger or to be moving slower. These are natural results of true focus.)

But seeing the ball better is only a partial benefit of focusing on its seams. Because the pattern made by the spinning ball is so subtle, it tends to engross the mind more completely. The mind is so absorbed in watching the pattern that it forgets to try too hard. To the extent that the mind is preoccupied with the seams, it tends not to interfere with the natural movements of the body. Furthermore, the seams are always here and now, and if the mind is on them it is kept from wandering to the past or future. The practice of this exercise will enable the tennis player to achieve deeper and deeper states of concentration.

Most players who practice seam-watching as a discipline find it helpful almost immediately, but after a while they often discover their minds wandering again. The mind has difficulty focusing on a single object for an extended period of time. Let's face it: as interesting as a tennis ball may be for some, it is not going to easily capture the restless mind, so habituated to distractions of every kind.

Bounce-Hit

So the question arises as to how to maintain focus for extended periods of time. The best way is to allow yourself to get interested in the ball. How do you do this? By not thinking you already know all about it, no matter how many thousands of balls you have seen in your life. Not assuming you already know is a powerful principle of focus.

One thing you don't know about the ball is exactly when it is going to bounce and when it is going to hit either your racket or your opponent's. Perhaps the most simple and effective means of focus I found was a very simple exercise I called "Bounce-Hit."

The instructions I gave students were very simple. "Say the word *bounce* out loud the instant you see the ball hit the court and the word *hit* the instant the ball makes contact with the racket— either racket." Saying the words out loud gave both me and the student the chance to hear whether the words were simultaneous with the events of bounce and hit. As the student said "bounce . . . hit . . . bounce . . . hit . . . bounce . . . hit . . . bounce . . . ," not only would it keep his eyes focused on four very key positions of the ball during each exchange, but the hearing of the rhythm and cadence of the bouncing and hitting of the ball seemed to hold the attention for longer periods of time.

The results were the same as with any effective focus. The exercise would give the player better feedback from the ball and, at the same time, help clear his mind of distractions. It's hard to be saying "bounce-hit" and at the same time overinstructing yourself, trying too hard or worrying about the score.

I found that beginners would learn effective footwork and beginning-level strokes and often be able to carry on quite long exchanges from the baseline within fifteen or twenty minutes without even thinking about it, while Self 1 was kept busy tracking the bounces and hits. Surprisingly I also found that many advanced players had more difficulty with the exercise, because they had more going on in their minds that they thought was necessary to good execution. When they would try the experiment of letting go of their controlling thoughts and just focus on the bounce and hit, they were usually very surprised and sometimes a little embarrassed about how well Self 2 performed without the usual kinds of Self 1 thought processes that they had felt were contributing so much to their game.

One of the easiest ways to maintain interest in the ball is to not look at it as a stationary object, but as an object in motion. Watching its seams helps focus your attention on the object itself, but it is just as important to increase your awareness of the *flight* of each ball as it moves toward you, and then again as it leaves your racket. My favorite focus of attention during a point is on the particular trajectories of each shot, both mine and my opponent's. I notice the height of the ball as it passes over the net, its apparent speed and with utmost care the angle at which it rises after bouncing. I also observe whether the ball is rising, falling or at its apex in the instant before the racket makes contact. I give the same careful attention to the trajectory of my own shot. Soon I become more and more aware of the rhythm of the alternating shots of each point, and am able to increase my sense of anticipation. It is this rhythm, both seen and heard, which holds fascination for my mind and enables it to focus for longer periods of time without becoming distracted.

Focus is not achieved by *staring* hard at something. It is not trying to force focus, nor does it mean thinking hard about something. Natural focus occurs when the mind is interested. When this occurs, the mind is drawn irresistibly toward the object (or subject) of interest. It is effortless and relaxed, not tense and overly controlled. When watching the tennis ball, allow yourself to fall into focus. If your eyes are squinting or straining, you are trying too hard. If you find yourself chastising yourself for losing focus, then you may be overcontrolling. Let the ball attract your mind, and both it and your muscles will stay appropriately relaxed.

LISTENING TO THE BALL

It rarely occurs to a player to listen to the ball, but I have found great value in this focus. When the ball hits your racket, it makes a distinct sound, the quality of which varies considerably, depending on its proximity to the "sweet spot," the angle of the face, the distribution of your weight and where the ball is met. If you listen closely to the sounds of one ball after another, you will soon be able to distinguish a number of different kinds and qualities of sounds. Soon it will be possible to recognize the sound produced by an overspin forehand hit squarely and an underspin forehand hit slightly off center. You will come to know the sound of a flat backhand, and to distinguish it from one hit with an open face.

One day when I was practicing this form of concentration while serving, I began hitting the ball unusually well. I could hear a sharp crack instead of the usual sound at the moment of impact.

It sounded terrific, and the ball had more speed and accuracy. After I realized how well I was serving, I resisted the temptation to figure out why, and simply asked my body to do whatever was necessary to reproduce that "crack." I held the sound in my memory, and to my amazement my body reproduced it time and again.

Through this experience I learned how effective the remembering of certain sounds can be as a cue for the built-in computer within our brains. While one listens to the sounds of his forehand, he can hold in his memory the sound that results from solid contact; as a result, the body will tend to repeat the elements of behavior which produced that sound. This technique can be particularly useful in learning the different kinds of serves. There is a distinct difference in the sounds of a flat, slice and twist serve. Similarly, one can learn to achieve the desired amount of spin in a second serve by listening closely to the sounds of balls hit with varying amounts of spin. Further, listening to the sound of the ball when volleying can improve both volley footwork and racket work. When a volley is met squarely at just the right moment, the action produces a wonderfully memorable sound.

Some players find the sound of the ball more mind-absorbing than watching the seams because it is something they've never done before. Actually there is no reason why both means of concentration cannot be employed on each shot, since one need listen only at the instant of contact.

I have found that the practice of listening to the ball is best used during practice. If you become sensitive to sound in practice, you will find that you will then use sound automatically during a match to encourage the repetition of solid shots. The habit will increase the number of balls hit solidly.

FEELING

When I was twelve years old, I heard my pro say of my doubles partner, "He really knows where his racket head is." I didn't know what he meant, but I intuited its importance and never forgot the remark. Few players understand the importance of concentrating attention on the *feel* of the racket as they are holding it. There are two things that a player *must* know on every shot: where the ball is and where his racket is. If he loses contact with either of these he is in trouble. Most players have learned to put visual attention on the ball, but many have only the vaguest notion about where their racket head is most of the time. The critical time to know the position of the racket is when it is behind you, and this requires concentration through the sense of feel.

On the forehand your hand is over a foot from the center of your racket. This means that even a tiny change in the angle of your wrist can produce a significant difference in the position of the center of the racket. Similarly, the slightest change in the angle of the face of the racket can have a substantial effect on the trajectory of the ball. In fact, if the face is off by only a quarter of an inch, the ball could travel over six feet out when hitting baseline to baseline. Hence, to achieve consistency and accuracy, you must become extraordinarily sensitive to feel.

It would be useful for all tennis players to undergo some "sensitivity training" with their bodies. The easiest way to get such training is simply to focus your attention on your body during practice. Ideally, someone should throw balls to you, or hit them so that they bounce in approximately the same spot each time. Then, paying relatively little attention to the ball, you can experience what it feels like to hit balls the way you hit them. You should spend some time merely feeling the exact path of your racket on your backswing. The greatest attention should be placed on the feel of your arm and hand at the moment just before they swing forward to meet the ball. Also become sensitive to how the handle feels in your hand. How hard are you squeezing your grip?

There are many ways to increase one's awareness of muscle feel. One is to take each of your strokes in slow motion. Each can be performed as an exercise, in which all attention is placed on the feel of the moving parts of the body. Get to know the feel of every inch of your stroke, every muscle in your body. Then when you increase your stroke speed to normal and begin hitting, you may be particularly aware of certain muscles. For instance, when I hit my best backhands, I am aware that my shoulder muscle, rather than my forearm, is pulling my arm through. By remembering the feel of that muscle before hitting a backhand, I attain the full benefit of the power it generates. Similarly, on my forehand I am particularly aware of my triceps when my racket is below the ball. By becoming sensitive to the feel of that muscle, I decrease my tendency to take my racket back too high.

It is also valuable to become more aware of rhythm. You can greatly improve your power and timing merely by paying attention during practice to the rhythm with which you hit each of your strokes. Every player has a rhythm natural to himself. If you learn to concentrate on the sense of rhythm, it is not difficult to fall into the rhythm most natural and effective for you. Rhythm can never be achieved by being overly purposeful about it; you have to let it happen. But sensitivity to rhythm developed through concentration helps. Those who have practiced concentrating on the feel of the path of their racket usually find that without intentional effort their stroke begins to slow down and to simplify. Both the rapid jerks and the fancy stuff tend to disappear and consistency and power tend to increase.

Just as it is helpful to become more aware of the sound of the ball, it is also useful to practice focusing on the feel of the ball at impact. You can notice subtle and not so subtle differences in the vibration sent up your hand when the ball strikes the racket, depending on where contact is made, your distribution of weight and the angle of the face of your racket. Again, you can program the best results by remembering as precisely as possible the feel in your hand, wrist and arm after a good solid hit. Practicing this kind of feel develops what is called "touch," and is particularly beneficial in hitting drop shots and lobs.

In short, become aware of your body. Know what it feels like to move your body into position, as well as how it feels to swing your racket. Remember: it is almost impossible to feel or see anything well if you are *thinking* about how you *should* be moving. Forget should's and experience *is*. In tennis there are only one or two elements to be aware of visually, but there are many things to feel. Expanding sensory knowledge of your body will greatly speed the process of developing skill.

In the last few pages, I have discussed ways of sharpening three of the five senses and expanding the awareness which is received through them. Practice them not as a list of tennis do's and don'ts, but one at a time and at your own rhythm.

As far as I know, taste and smell are not crucial to successful tennis. You can practice these if you like during your meal after your tennis match.

THE THEORY OF CONCENTRATION

The practices mentioned above can speed learning to play your best tennis. But we have come to an important point that should not be passed over quickly. Though focus of attention helps your tennis, it is equally true that playing tennis can help your focus of attention. Learning focus of attention is a master skill that has unlimited application. For those interested, let me elaborate briefly on some theoretical aspects of concentration.

Whatever we experience on a tennis court is known to us by virtue of awareness—that is, by the consciousness within us. It is consciousness which makes possible awareness of the sights, sounds, feelings and thoughts which compose what we call "experience." It is self-evident that one cannot experience anything *outside* of consciousness. Consciousness is that which makes all things and events knowable. Without consciousness eyes could not see, ears could not hear, and mind could not think. Consciousness is like a pure light energy whose power is to make events knowable, just as an electric light makes objects visible. Consciousness could be called the light of lights because it is by its light that all other lights become visible.

In the human body the light energy of consciousness does its knowing through several limited facilities—namely, the five senses and the mind. Through eyes, it knows sights; through ears, sounds; and through mind it knows concepts, facts and ideas. All that ever happens to us, all that we ever do, is known to us through the light energy of what is called consciousness.

Right now your consciousness is aware through your eyes and mind of the words in this sentence. But other things are also happening within the range of your attention. If you stop to listen closely to whatever your ears can hear, you will no doubt be able to hear sounds which you previously weren't aware of, even though they were going on while you were reading. If you now listen to these sounds closely, you will hear them better—that is, you will be able to know them better. Probably you were not aware of how your tongue feels in your mouth—but in all likelihood after reading the foregoing words, you now are. While you were reading or listening to the sights and sounds around you, you were not aware of the feeling of your tongue, but with the slightest suggestion, the mind directs the focus of attention from one thing to another. When attention is allowed to focus, it comes to know that place. Attention is focused consciousness, and consciousness is that power of knowing.

Consider this analogy. If consciousness were like an electric light shining in a dark forest, by virtue of this light, it would be possible to see and know the forest within a certain radius. The closer an object is to the light, the more it will be illuminated and the greater the detail that will be visible. Objects farther away are seen more vaguely. But if we put a reflector around this light, making it into a searchlight, then all the light would shine in one direction. Now objects that are in the path of the light will be seen with greater clarity and many objects which were previously "lost in darkness" will become knowable. This is the power of focus of attention. If, however, the lens of the searchlight was dirty, or there were bubbles in the glass that diffracted the light, or if the light was oscillating, then the beam would be dispersed, and some focus would be lost and with it clarity. Distraction is then like dirt on the lens of the light or like the light jerking around so quickly that illumination is effectively reduced.

The light of consciousness can be focused either externally to objects available to the senses or internally to thoughts or feelings. And attention can be focused in a broad or narrow beam. Broad focus would be an attempt to see as much of the forest at one time as possible. Narrow focus would be directing attention to something very specific like the veins on a particular leaf on a particular twig of a branch.

THE HERE AND NOW OF THE TENNIS COURT

Back to the tennis court. Watching the seams of the ball is a narrow focus of attention, and can be effective in blocking out nervousness and other possible irrelevant objects of attention. Sensing the feel of your body is a broader focus, and takes in a number of sensations that might aid in the learning of tennis. To take in the wind, the movement of your opponent, the trajectory of the ball and the sensations in your body is an even broader focus, but perhaps quite relevant to the task at hand. It is still focus because it leaves out all that is irrelevant, and illuminates all that is relevant. One thing that can be said about focus is that it is always here and now—that is, in present time and present space. The first part of this chapter suggested several "here"s as objects of concentration. The seams focus awareness more exactly in space than merely the ball itself does, and as you add awareness of one element of the game of tennis after another—from the sound of the ball to the feel of each part of each stroke—greater knowledge is gained.

But it is also necessary to learn to focus awareness in the *now*. This simply means tuning in to what is happening in the present. The greatest lapses in concentration come when we allow our minds to project what is about to happen or to dwell on what has already happened. How easily the mind absorbs itself in the world of "what if"s. "What if I lose this point?" it thinks; "then I'll be behind 5–3 on his serve. If I don't break his serve, then I'll have lost the first set and probably the match. I wonder what Martha will say when she hears I lost to George." At this point it is not uncommon for the mind to lapse into a little fantasy about Martha's reaction to hearing the news that you have lost to George. Meanwhile, back in the now, the score is still 3–4, 30–40, and you are barely aware that you are on the court; the conscious energy you need to perform at your peak in the now has been leaking into an imagined future.

Similarly, the mind often draws one's attention into the past. "If the linesman hadn't called that last serve out, the score would be deuce and I wouldn't be in this mess. The same thing happened to me last week, and it cost me the match. It made me lose my confidence, and now the same thing is happening again. I wonder why." One nice aspect of tennis is that before long you or your opponent is going to hit a ball, and this will summon you back to the present. But usually part of our energy is left in the thought world of past or future, so that the present is not seen in the light of one's full awareness. As a result, objects look dim, the ball seems to come faster, appears smaller, and even the court seems to shrink.

Since the mind seems to have a will of its own, how can one learn to keep it in the present? By practice. There is no other way. Every time your mind starts to leak away, simply bring it gently back. I used to use a ball machine with a wide range in velocity, and had a simple drill which helped players experience what it means to be more in the present. I asked students to stand at net in the volley position, and then set the machine to shoot balls at three-quarter speed. From being initially casual, they suddenly became more alert. At first the balls seemed too fast for them, but soon their responses quickened. Gradually I turned the machine to faster and faster speeds, and the volleyers became more focused. When they were responding quickly enough to hit the top-speed balls and believed they were at the peak of their concentration, I moved the machine to midcourt, fifteen feet closer than before. At this point students would often lose some concentration as a degree of fear intruded. Their forearms would tense slightly, making their movements less quick and accurate. "Relax your forearm. Relax your mind. Simply relax into the present, focus on the seams of the ball, and let it happen." Soon they were again able to meet the ball in front of them with the center of their rackets. There was no smile of self-satisfaction, merely total absorption in each moment. Afterward some players said that the ball seemed to slow down; others remarked how weird it was to hit balls when you didn't have time to think about it. All who enter even a little into that state of being present will experience a calmness and a degree of ecstasy which they will want to repeat.

The practical consequences to your volley of increasing your alertness are obvious. Most volleys are missed either because contact is made too far behind the player, or because they are off center. Becoming more aware of the present makes it easier to know where the ball is at all times and to react soon enough to meet it at the instant of your choice. Some people think that they are just too slow to return a hard shot when they are at net. But time is a relative thing, and it really *is* possible to slow it down. Consider: there are 1000 milliseconds in every second. That's a lot of milliseconds. Alertness is a measure of how many nows you are alert to in a given period. The result is simple: you become more aware of what is going on as you learn to keep your attention in the now.

After practicing being present to the moment, I found that I could change my position on the return of serve from standing at the baseline to standing only a foot behind the service line. If I stayed focused and relaxed, I could see even fast serves well enough to "slow them down in time," respond and pick up the ball just a split second after it bounced. There was no time for a backswing and no time to think about what I was doing or even where I would hit the ball. There would just be a calm focus and a spontaneous response to meet the ball and follow-through, giving depth and direction to the ball. At the next instant I would be at the net—well before the server!

The server, seeing me standing at the service line to receive his serve, would have to deal mentally with what he might take to be an insult to his serve; he would often double-fault more than once in an effort to teach me a lesson. His next problem would be hitting a volley passing shot from somewhere within no man's land.

The reader might quite naturally think that this tactic would be impossible against a really first-rate serve. Not true. After only a few months of experimenting with this return of serve, I found it possible to use it to great advantage in tournament play. The more I used it, the quicker and more accurate my reactions became. Concentration seemed to slow time down, giving me the necessary awareness to see and place the ball. The fact that I met the ball on the rise cut off all the angle that a server usually gets on his serve after it bounces. And the fact that I could reach the net before the server gave me control of the commanding position on the court.

FOCUS DURING A MATCH

Most of the ways for developing concentration mentioned earlier are best employed during practice. In a match it is usually best to pick one focus—whatever works best for you—and stick with it. For example, if the seams of the ball tend to keep you centered in the here and now, there is no need to focus on sound or feel. Often the fact that you are playing a match will help you to focus. During the course of a point, you often find yourself in a state of relatively deep concentration in which you are only aware of what is happening at that instant. The critical time is between points! After the last shot of a rally, the mind leaves its focus on the ball and is free to wander. It is at this moment that thoughts about the score, your erratic backhand, business, the children, dinner and so forth tend to siphon your energy away from the here and now. Then it is difficult to regain the same level of concentration before the next point begins.

How to stay concentrated in the here and now between points? My own device, and one that has been effective for many of my students, is to focus attention on breathing. Some object or activity which is always present is needed. What is more here and now than one's breathing? Putting attention on breathing simply means observing my breath going in, going out, going in, going out in its natural rhythm. It does *not* mean intentionally controlling my breath.

Breathing is a remarkable phenomenon. Whether we intend to or not, we breathe. Awake or asleep, it is always happening. Even if we try to stop, some force will soon overpower our efforts and we will take a breath. Thus, when we focus on breathing we are putting our attention on something closely connected to the life energy of the body. Also, breathing is a very basic rhythm. It is said that in breathing man recapitulates the rhythm of the universe. When the mind is fastened to the rhythm of breathing, it tends to become absorbed and calm. Whether on or off the court, I know of no better way to begin to deal with anxiety than to place the mind on one's breathing process. Anxiety is fear about what may happen in the future, and it occurs only when the mind is imagining what the future may bring. But when your attention is on the here and now, the actions which need to be done in the present have their best chance of being successfully accomplished, and as a result the future will become the best possible present.

So after a point has ended and I'm returning to position or going to pick up a ball, I place my mind on my breathing. The second my mind starts wondering about whether I'm going to win or lose the match, I bring it gently back to my breath and relax in its natural and basic motion. In this way, by the time the next point is ready to start, I am able to be even more concentrated than I was in the midst of the previous one. This technique is not only useful for me in stopping the mind from fretting about bad shots, but keeps me from being self-conscious about unusually good shots.

PLAYING IN SELF 2'S ZONE

In the first chapter of this book I referred to the ways people tend to describe their state of mind when they are playing their best tennis. They used to use such phrases as "playing out of my mind" or "playing over his head." The current phrase is "playing in the zone." The interesting fact about this state of mind is that it really cannot be described accurately because at the moment you are in that state, the one that usually describes is not present. After you are out of the state, you may try to remember what it was like. But it is hard. All you may know is that it felt good and it worked like magic.

However, even though you don't know much about what is happening in that state, you can know a lot about what is not happening. You can remember that you weren't criticizing yourself; you weren't congratulating yourself either. You weren't thinking about how to do the stroke correctly or how not to do the stroke. You were not thinking about past shots or about the future score, about what people would think or even about the results to be obtained. In other words what was missing was Self 1. What was left was Self 2. Because Self 1 is not in the picture, sometimes we say, I didn't do it, it just happened. Commonly students use language like, "I wasn't there," "Something else took over," "My racket did this, or did that," as if it had a will of its own. But the racket wasn't missing, and the great shot was not an accident, even though you didn't plan it. It was Self 2 hitting the ball. It was in fact *you* hitting the ball without the normal interference from Self 1.

Interestingly, this state of being, when Self 1 is absent and Self 2 is present, always feels good, and allows a more vivid consciousness and usually great excellence in performance. It may not feel the same as ego gratification, a feeling which we all too often like a great deal, but there is a feeling some call harmony, balance, poise, even peace, or contentment. And it can feel that way in the middle of a very "intense" tennis match.

Phil Jackson, coach of Michael Jordan and the four-time NBA Champions, the Chicago Bulls, describes the state of Self 2 focus very well in his book, *Sacred Hoops:* "Basketball is a complex dance that requires shifting from one objective to another at lightning speed. To excel, you need to act with a clear mind and be totally focused on what everyone on the floor is doing. The secret is not thinking. That doesn't mean being stupid; it means quieting the endless jabbering of thoughts so that your body can do instinctively what it's been trained to do without the mind getting in the way. All of us have flashes of oneness . . . When we're completely immersed in the moment, inseparable from what we're doing."

I was reading a description of the zone by Bill Russell, the famous basketball player for the Boston Celtics: "At that special level all sorts of odd things happened. . . . It was almost as if we were playing in slow motion. During those spells I could almost sense how the next play would develop and where the next shot would be taken. Even before the other team brought the ball in bounds, I could feel it so keenly that I'd want to shout to my teammates, 'It's coming there!'—except that I knew everything would change if I did. My premonitions would be consistently correct, and I always felt then that I not only knew all the Celtics by heart but also all the opposing players, and that they all knew me. It seems less odd to me now. It seems more like, yes, that's the way it is, that's the way it should be all the time. We can be focused. We can be conscious."

One caution about "the zone": it cannot be controlled by Self 1. I have seen many articles that claim to provide a technique for "playing in the zone every time." Forget it! This is a setup. It's an age-old trap. Self 1 likes the *idea* of playing in the zone, especially the results that usually occur. So Self 1 will try to grasp onto almost anything that promises to take you to what everyone agrees is a wonderful place. But there is one catch; the only way to get there is to leave Self 1 behind. So as long as you let Self 1 be the one that takes you there, it will be there too and you will not be able to go into the zone. If you do, even for a moment, Self 1 will say, "Good, I got there," and you will be out again.

Another way to look at the zone is that it comes as a gift. It is not a gift you can demand of yourself, but one you can ask for. How do you ask? By making your effort? What is your effort?

Your effort depends on your understanding. But I would say it always involves an effort to focus and an effort to let go of Self 1 control. As trust increases, Self 1 quiets, Self 2 becomes more conscious and more present, enjoyment increases and the gifts are being given. If you are willing to give credit where credit is due and not think you "know" how to do it, the gifts are apt to be more frequent and sustainable.

This may not sound scientific, or may not sound as in control as you might like. But I can say that I've been courting Self 2 for a long time now, over twenty-five years consciously, and it comes at its own timing, when I am ready for it—humble, respectful, not expecting it, somehow placing myself lower than it, not above it. Then when the moment is right, it comes, and I can enjoy the absence of Self 1 thought and the presence of joy. I like it a lot. Grab for it, and it will squirt away like a slippery bar of soap. Take it for granted, and you will be distracted and lose it. I used to think that whatever was present in that state would leave me, was ephemeral. Now I know that it is always there and it is only I who leave. When I look at a young child I realize it is there all the time. As the child grows, there is more to distract the mind, and it is harder to recognize. But it, Self 2, may be the only thing which has been there and will be there your entire life. Thoughts and thinking come and go, but the child self, the true self, is there and will be there as long as our breath is. To enjoy it, to appreciate it, is the gift of focus.

LAPSES IN FOCUS

It is perplexing to wonder why we ever leave the here and now. Here and now are the only place and time when one ever enjoys himself or accomplishes anything. Most of our suffering takes place when we allow our minds to imagine the future or mull over the past. Nonetheless, few people are ever satisfied with what is before them at the moment. Our desire that things be different from what they are pulls our minds into an unreal world, and consequently we are less able to appreciate what the present has to offer. Our minds leave the reality of the present only when we prefer the unreality of the past or future. To begin to understand my own lapses of concentration I had to know what I was really desiring, and it soon became clear to me that there were more desires operating in me on the court than simply to play tennis. In other words, tennis was not the only game I was playing on the court. Part of the process of attaining a concentrated state of mind is to know and resolve these conflicting desires; the following chapter attempts to shed light on this process.

EIGHT

Games People Play
on the Court

THAT SOMETHING ELSE BESIDES TENNIS IS BEING PLAYED ON THE courts is obvious to the most casual observer. Regardless of whether he is watching the game at a country club, a public park or a private court, he will see players suffering everything from minor frustration to major exasperation. He will see the stomping of feet, shaking of fists, war dances, rituals, pleas, oaths and prayers; rackets are thrown against fences in anger, into the air for joy, or pounded against the concrete in disgust. Balls that are in will be called out, and vice versa. Linesmen are threatened, ball boys scolded and the integrity of friends questioned. On the faces of players you may observe, in quick succession, shame, pride, ecstasy and despair. Smug complacency gives way to high anxiety, cockiness to hangdog disappointment. Anger and aggression of varying intensity are expressed both openly and in disguised forms. If an observer was watching the game for the first time, it would be hard for him to believe that all this drama could be contained on a mere tennis court, between love-all and game, set and match.

There is no end to the variety of attitudes toward the game. Not only can the full spectrum of emotional response be observed on the court, but also a wide range in the motivations of its players. Some care only about winning. Some are amazingly tenacious about warding off defeat, but can't win a match point if it's offered to them. Many don't care how they play, just as long as they look good, and some simply don't care at all. Some cheat their opponents; others cheat themselves. Some are always bragging about how good they are; others constantly tell you how poorly they are playing. There are even a small handful who are out on the court simply for fun and exercise.

In his widely read book, *Games People Play*, Eric Berne described the subliminal games that lie beneath the surface of human interaction. He made it remarkably clear that what *appears* to be happening between people is only a small part of the story. The same seems to be true on the tennis court, and since, to play any game well, one must know as much as possible about it, I include here a brief guide to the games people play on the tennis court, followed by a brief account of my own search for a game worth playing. I suggest that this guide be read not as an exercise in self-analysis, but as a key to discovering how to have more fun while playing tennis. It's difficult to have fun or to achieve concentration when your ego is engaged in what it thinks is a life-and-death struggle. Self 2 will never be allowed to express spontaneity and excellence when Self 1 is playing some heavy ulterior game involving its self-image. Yet as one recognizes the games of Self 1, a degree of freedom can be achieved. When it is, you can discriminate objectively and discover for yourself the game you think is really worth playing.

A brief explanation of the meaning of "game." Every game involves at least one player, a goal, some obstacle between the player and his goal, a field (physical or mental) on which the game is played and a motive for playing.

In the guide below I have named three categories of games with their aims and motives for playing. I call these games Good-o, Friends-o and Health-o–Fun-o, and they are played both on and off the courts. Under each of these major categories are sub-games, which have subaims and submotivations, and even each subgame has numerous variations. Moreover, most people play hybrid forms of two or three games at a time.

Main Game 1: Good-o

GENERAL AIM: To Achieve Excellence
GENERAL MOTIVE: To Prove Oneself "Good"

Subgame A: Perfect-o
Thesis: How good can I get? In Perfect-o, "good" is measured against a standard of performance. In golf, it is measured against par; in tennis, against self-conceived expectations or those of parents, coach or friends.
Aim: Perfection; to reach the highest standard possible.
Motive: The desire to prove oneself.
Obstacles:
External: The never-closing gap between one's idea of perfection and one's apparent abilities.
Internal: Self-criticism for not being as close to perfection as one would like, leading to discouragement, compulsively trying too hard and the self-doubt that made you think you had anything to prove in the first place.

Subgame B: Compete-o
Thesis: I'm better than you. Here, "good" is measured against the performance of other players rather than against a set standard.
Maxim: It's not how well I play, but whether I win or lose that counts.
Aim: To be the best; to win; to defeat all comers.

MOTIVE: Desire to be at the top of the heap. Stems from need for admiration and control.

OBSTACLES:

External: There is always someone around who can beat you; the rising ability of the young.

Internal: The mind's preoccupation with comparing oneself with others, thus preventing spontaneous action; thoughts of inferiority alternating with superiority, depending on the competition; fear of defeat.

SUBGAME C: Image-o

THESIS: Look at me! "Good" is measured by appearance. Neither winning nor true competence is as important as style.

AIM: To look good, flashy, strong, brilliant, smooth, graceful.

MOTIVE: Desire for attention, praise.

OBSTACLES:

External: One can never look good enough. What looks good to one person does not look so good to another.

Internal: Confusion about who one really is. Fear of not pleasing everyone and of imagined loneliness.

Main Game 2: Friends-o

GENERAL AIM: To Make or Keep Friends

GENERAL MOTIVE: Desire for Friendship

SUBGAME A: Status-o

THESIS: We play at the country club. It's not so important how good you are as where you play and who plays with you.

AIM: To maintain or improve social status.

MOTIVE: Desire for the friendship of the prominent.

OBSTACLES:

External: The cost of keeping up with the Joneses.

Internal: Fear of losing one's social position.

SUBGAME B: Togetherness-o

THESIS: All my good friends play tennis. You play to be with your friends. To play too well would be a mistake.

AIM: To meet or keep friends.
MOTIVE: Desire for acceptance and friendship.
OBSTACLES:
External: Finding the time, the place and the friends.
Internal: Fear of ostracism.

SUBGAME C: Husband-o or Wife-o
THESIS: My husband (or wife) is always playing, so . . .
AIM: To see your spouse.
MOTIVE: Loneliness.
OBSTACLES:
External: Becoming good enough for spouse to play with you.
Internal: Doubts that loneliness can be overcome on the tennis court. (See also internal obstacles of Perfect-o.)

Main Game 3: Health-o–Fun-o

GENERAL AIM: Mental or Physical Health or Pleasure
GENERAL MOTIVE: Health and/or Fun

SUBGAME A: Health-o
THESIS: Played on doctor's advice, or as part of self-initiated physical improvement or beautification program.
AIM: Exercise, work up a sweat, relax the mind.
MOTIVE: Health, vitality, desire for prolongation of youth.
OBSTACLES:
External: Finding someone of like motive to play with.
Internal: Doubts that tennis is really helping. The temptation to be drawn into Perfect-o or Good-o.

SUBGAME B: Fun-o
THESIS: Played neither for winning nor to become "good," but for fun alone. (A game rarely played in its pure form.)
AIM: To have as much fun as possible.
MOTIVE: The enjoyment, in expression of excellence.
OBSTACLES:
External: None.
Internal: Being pulled into Self 1 games.

SUBGAME C: Learn-o
THESIS: Played out of Self 2's desire to learn and grow.
AIM: Evolve.
MOTIVE: Enjoyment of learning.
OBSTACLES:
External: None.
Internal: Tendency to be drawn into Self 1 games.

These three subgames can all be played at once without interfering with each other. They are internally harmonious with Self 2's innate desires.

THE COMPETITIVE ETHIC
AND THE RISE OF GOOD-O

Many "serious" tennis players in our society, regardless of the reasons which they may think motivated them to take up the sport in the first place, end up playing one or another version of Good-o. Many start tennis as a weekend sport in the hope of getting exercise and a needed relief from the pressures of daily life, but they end by setting impossible standards of excellence for themselves and often become more frustrated and tense on the court than off it.

How can the quality of one's tennis assume such importance that it causes anxiety, anger, depression and self-doubt? The answer seems to be deeply rooted in a basic pattern of our culture. We live in an achievement-oriented society where people tend to be measured by their competence in various endeavors. Even before we received praise or blame for our first report card, we were loved or ignored for how well we performed our very first actions. From this pattern, one basic message came across loud, clear and often: you are a good person and worthy of respect only if you do things successfully. Of course, the kind of things needed to be done well to deserve love varies from family to family, but the underlying equation between self-worth and performance has been nearly universal.

Now, that's a pretty heavy equation, for it means that to some extent every achievement-oriented action becomes a criterion for defining one's self-worth.

If someone plays bad golf, it comes somehow to mean that he is not quite as worthy of respect, his own or others', as he would be if he played well. If he is the club champion, he is considered a winner, and thus a more valuable person in our society. It then follows that the intelligent, beautiful and competent tend to regard themselves as *better* people.

When love and respect depend on winning or doing well in a competitive society, it is inevitable (since every winner requires a loser and every top performance many inferior ones) that there will be many people who feel a lack of love and respect. Of course, these people will try hard to win the respect they lack, and the winners will try equally hard not to lose the respect they have won. In this light, it is not difficult to see why playing well has come to mean so much to us.

But who said that I am to be measured by how well I do things? In fact, who said that I should be measured at all? Who indeed? What is required to disengage oneself from this trap is a clear knowledge that the value of a human being cannot be measured by performance—or by any other arbitrary measurement. Do we really think the value of a human being is measurable? It doesn't really make sense to measure ourselves in comparison with other immeasurable beings. In fact, we are what we are; we are *not* how well we happen to perform at a given moment. The grade on a report card may measure an ability in arithmetic, but it doesn't measure the person's value. Similarly, the score of a tennis match may be an indication of how well I performed or how hard I tried, but it does not define me, nor give me cause to consider myself as something more or less than I was before the match.

MY SEARCH FOR A GAME WORTH PLAYING

At about the age I was tall enough to see over the net, my father started me on tennis. I played the game more or less casually with my cousins and older sister until I was eleven, when I received my first tennis lesson from a new pro named John Gardiner at Pebble Beach, California. That same year, I played in my first tournament in the "under 11" division of the National Hardcourt Championships. The night before the match, I dreamed of the glory of being a dark-horse winner. My first match was a nervous but easy victory. My second, against the second-seeded player, ended in a 6–3, 6–4 defeat and with me sobbing bitterly. I had no idea why winning meant so much to me.

The next few summers I played tennis every day. I would wake myself at 7 A.M., make and eat my own breakfast in five minutes, then run miles to the Pebble Beach courts. I usually arrived a good hour before anyone else and would spend the time hitting forehands and backhands tirelessly against a backboard. During the day, I would play ten or fifteen sets, drill and take lessons, not stopping until there was no longer enough light to see the ball. Why? I really didn't know. If someone had asked, I would have said that it was because I liked tennis. Though this was partially true, it was primarily because I was deeply involved in the game of Perfect-o. There was something I seemed to want badly to prove to myself. Winning was important to me in tournaments, but playing well was important day by day; I wanted to get better and better. My style was to think I would never win, and then to try to surprise myself and others. I was hard to beat, but I had an equally difficult time winning close matches. Though I hated losing, I didn't really enjoy beating someone else; I found it slightly embarrassing. I was a tirelessly hard worker and never stopped trying to improve my strokes.

By the time I was fifteen I had won the National Hardcourt Championship in the boys' division, and felt the rush of excitement at winning a major tournament. Earlier the same summer I went to the National Championships at Kalamazoo and lost in the quarterfinals to the seventh-seeded player 3–6, 6–0, 10–8. In the last set, I had been ahead 5–3, 40–15 on my serve. I was nervous but optimistic. In the first match point, I double-faulted in an attempt to serve an ace on my second serve. In the second, I missed the easiest put-away volley possible in front of a packed grandstand. For many years thereafter, I replayed that match point in countless dreams, and it is as vivid in my memory now as it was on that day twenty years ago. Why? What difference did it really make? It didn't occur to me to ask.

By the time I entered college, I had given up the idea of proving my worth through the vehicle of championship tennis, and was happy to settle for being "a good amateur." I put most of my energy into intellectual endeavors, sometimes grade-grubbing, sometimes a sincere search for Truth. From my sophomore year onward I played varsity tennis, and found that on days when I did poorly in my academic work, I would usually perform badly also on the tennis court. I would try hard to prove on the court what I had difficulty proving scholastically, but would usually find that lack of confidence in the one area tended to infect the other. Fortunately, the reverse was also true. During four years of collegiate play, I was almost always nervous when I walked onto a court to play a match. By the time I was a senior and had been elected captain of the team, I was of the intellectual opinion that competition really didn't prove anything—but I was still tight before most matches.

After graduation I gave up competitive tennis for ten years and embarked on a career in education. While teaching English at Exeter Academy in New Hampshire, I realized that even the smartest of kids interfered significantly with their ability to learn and perform academically. Then, while a training officer on the U.S.S. *Topeka*, I saw how impoverished was our system of education and how backward our methods of training. When I got out of the Navy, I joined a group of idealists to found a liberal arts college in Northern Michigan. During its short five years of existence, I became more and more interested in learning how to learn and how to help others learn. I studied the work of Abraham Maslow and Carl Rogers in the late sixties, and studied learning theory at Claremont Graduate School, but did not really make a practical breakthrough in learning until, while on sabbatical from "education," I taught tennis during the summer of 1970. I became interested in learning theory and, that summer, began to gain some insights into the learning process. Deciding to continue teaching tennis, I developed what came to be called the Inner Game—a way of learning that seemed to increase tremendously the learning rate of students. It also had a beneficial effect on my game. Learning a little about the art of concentration helped my game revive quickly, and soon I was consistently playing better than ever. After I became the club pro at the Meadowbrook Club in Seaside, California, I found that even though I didn't have much time to work on my own strokes, by applying the principles I was teaching I could maintain a game which was seldom defeated by anyone in the local area.

One day, after playing particularly well against a very good player, I began wondering how I might fare in tournament competition. I felt confident of my game; still, I hadn't played against ranked players. So I entered a tournament at the Berkeley Tennis Club in which top-ranking players were competing. On the appointed weekend, I drove to Berkeley with confidence, but by the time I arrived I had started to question my own ability. Everyone there seemed to be six foot five and to be carrying five or six rackets. I recognized many of the players from tennis magazines, but none of them seemed to recognize me. The atmosphere was very different from that of Meadowbrook, my little pond where I was chief frog. Suddenly I found my previous optimism turning to pessimism. I was doubting my game. Why? Had anything happened to it from the time I left my club three hours before?

My first match was against a player who literally *was* six foot five. Even though he carried only three rackets, as we each walked to a backcourt my knees felt a bit wobbly and my wrist didn't seem as strong as usual. I tested it several times, tightening my hand on the handle of my racket. I wondered what would happen out on the court. But when we began to warm up, I soon saw that my opponent wasn't nearly as good as I had imagined. Had I been giving him a lesson, I knew exactly what I would tell him, and I quickly categorized him as a "better-than-average club player" and felt better.

However, an hour later, with the score 4–1 in his favor in the second set, and having lost the first set 6–3, I began to realize that I was about to be beaten by a "better-than-average club player." All during the match I had been on edge, missing easy shots and playing inconsistently. It seemed my concentration was off just enough so that I missed lines by inches and hit the top of the net with every other volley.

As it worked out, my opponent, on the verge of a clear victory, faltered. I don't know what was happening inside his head, but he couldn't finish me off. He lost the second set 7–5 and the next 6–1, but as I walked off the court, I had no sense that I had won the match—rather, that he had lost it.

I began thinking immediately of my next match against a player highly ranked in northern California. I knew that he was a more experienced tournament player than I and probably more skilled. I certainly didn't want to play the way I had during the first round; it would be a rout. But my knees were still shaky, my mind didn't seem able to focus clearly, and I was nervous. Finally, I sat down in seclusion to see if I could come to grips with myself. I began by asking myself, "What's the worst that can happen?"

The answer was easy: "I could lose 6–0, 6–0."

"Well, what if you did? What then?"

"Well . . . I'd be out of the tournament and go back to Meadowbrook. People would ask me how I did, and I would say that I lost in the second round to So-and-So."

They'd say sympathetically, "Oh, he's pretty tough. What was the score?" Then I would have to confess; love and love.

"What would happen next?" I asked myself.

"Well, word would quickly get around that I had been trounced up at Berkeley, but soon I'd start playing well again and before long life would be back to normal."

I had tried to be as honest as I could about the worst possible results. They weren't good, but neither were they unbearable—certainly not bad enough to get upset about. Then I asked myself, "What's the best that could happen?"

Again the answer was clear: I could win 6–0, 6–0.

"Then what?"

"I'd have to play another match, and then another until I was beaten, which in a tournament like this was soon inevitable. Then I would return to my own club, report how I did, receive a few pats on the back, and soon all would again return to normal."

Staying in the tournament another round or two didn't seem overwhelmingly attractive, so I asked myself a final question: "Then what do you *really* want?"

The answer was quite unexpected. What I really wanted, I realized, was to overcome the nervousness that was preventing me from playing my best and enjoying myself. I wanted to overcome the inner obstacle that had plagued me for so much of my life. I wanted to win the *inner* game.

Having come to this realization, knowing what I really wanted, I walked toward my match with a new sense of enthusiasm. In the first game, I double-faulted three times and lost my serve, but from then on I felt a new certainty. It was as if a huge pressure had been relieved, and I was out there playing with all the energies at my command. As it worked out, I was never able to break my opponent's spinning, left-handed serve, but I didn't lose my own serve again until the last game in the second set. I had lost 6–4, 6–4, but I walked off the courts feeling that I had won. I had lost the external game, but had won the game I had wanted to, my *own* game, and I felt very happy. Indeed, when a friend came up to me after the match and asked how I'd done, I was tempted to say, "I won!"

For the first time I recognized the existence of the Inner Game, and its importance to me. I didn't know what the rules of the game were, nor exactly what its aim was, but I did sense that it involved something more than winning a trophy.

NINE

The Meaning
of Competition

IN CONTEMPORARY WESTERN CULTURE THERE IS A GREAT DEAL OF controversy about competition. One segment values it highly, believing that it is responsible for Western progress and prosperity. Another segment says that competition is bad; that it pits one person against another and is therefore divisive; that it leads to enmity between people and therefore to a lack of cooperation and eventual ineffectualness. Those who value competition believe in sports such as football, baseball, tennis and golf. Those who see competition as a form of legalized hostility tend to favor such noncompetitive forms of recreation as surfing, Frisbee or jogging. If they do play tennis or golf, they insist on doing it "noncompetitively." Their maxim is that cooperation is better than competition.

Those who argue against the value of competition have plenty of ammunition. As pointed out in the last chapter, there is a wealth of evidence showing how frenzied people tend to become in competitive situations. It is true that competition for many is merely an arena for venting aggression; it is taken as a proving ground for establishing who is the stronger, tougher or smarter. Each imagines that by beating the other he has in some way established his superiority over him, not just in a game, but as a person. What is seldom recognized is that the need to prove yourself is based on insecurity and self-doubt. Only to the extent that one is unsure about who and what he is does he need to prove himself to himself or to others.

It is when competition is thus used as a means of creating a self-image relative to others that the worst in a person tends to come out; then the ordinary fears and frustrations become greatly exaggerated. If I am secretly afraid that playing badly or losing the match may be taken to mean that I am less of a man, naturally I am going to be more upset with myself for missing shots. And, of course, this very uptightness will make it more difficult for me to perform at my highest levels. There would be no problem with competition if one's self-image were not at stake.

I have taught many children and teenagers who were caught up in the belief that their self-worth depended on how well they performed at tennis and other skills. For them, playing well and winning are often life-and-death issues. They are constantly measuring themselves in comparison with their friends by using their skill at tennis as one of the measuring rods. It is as if some believe that only by being the best, only by being a winner, will they be eligible for the love and respect they seek. Many parents foster this belief in their children. Yet in the process of learning to measure our value according to our abilities and achievements, the true and measureless value of each individual is ignored. Children who have been taught to measure themselves in this way often become adults driven by a compulsion to succeed which overshadows all else. The tragedy of this belief is not that they will fail to find the success they seek, but that they will not discover the love or even the self-respect they were led to believe will come with it. Furthermore, in their single-minded pursuit of measurable success, the development of many other human potentialities is sadly neglected. Some never find the time or inclination to appreciate the beauties of nature, to express their deepest feelings and thoughts to a loved one, or to wonder about the ultimate purpose of their existence.

But whereas some seem to get trapped in the compulsion to succeed, others take a rebellious stance. Pointing to the blatant cruelties and limitations involved in a cultural pattern which tends to value only the winner and ignore even the positive qualities of the mediocre, they vehemently criticize competition. Among the most vocal are youth who have suffered under competitive pressures imposed on them by parents or society. Teaching these young people, I often observe in them a desire to fail. They seem to seek failure by making no effort to win or achieve success. They go on strike, as it were. By not trying, they always have an alibi: "I may have lost, but it doesn't count because I really didn't try." What is not usually admitted is the belief that if they had really tried and lost, then yes, that *would* count. Such a loss would be a measure of their worth. Clearly this belief is the same as that of the competitor trying to prove himself. Both are Self 1 ego trips; both are based on the mistaken assumption that one's sense of self-respect rides on how well he performs in relation to others. Both show fear of not measuring up. Only as this fundamental and often nagging fear begins to dissolve can we discover a new meaning in competition.

My own attitude toward competition went through quite an evolution before I arrived at my present point of view. As described in the last chapter I was raised to believe in competition, and both playing well and winning meant a great deal to me. But as I began exploring Self 2's learning process in both the teaching and playing of tennis, I became noncompetitive. Instead of trying to win, I decided to attempt only to play beautifully and excellently; in other words, I began to play a rather pure form of Perfect-o. My theory was that I would be unconcerned with how well I was doing in relation to my opponent and absorbed solely in achieving excellence for its own sake. Very beautiful; I would waltz around the court being very fluid, accurate and "wise."

But something was missing. I didn't experience a desire to win, and as a result I often lacked the necessary determination. I had thought that it was in the desire to win that one's ego entered the picture, but at one point I began to ask myself if there wasn't such a motivation as an egoless desire to win. Was there a determination to win that wasn't an ego trip and didn't involve all the fears and frustrations that accompany ego trips? Does the will to win always have to mean "See, I'm better than you"?

One day I had an interesting experience which convinced me in an unexpected way that playing for the sake of beauty and excellence was not all there was to tennis. For several weeks I had been trying to get a date with a particular girl. She had turned me down twice, but each time with what appeared to be a good reason. Finally a dinner date was set, and on that day as I finished my last lesson one of the other pros asked me to play a couple of sets. "I'd really like to, Fred," I replied, "but I can't make it this evening." At that moment I was informed there was a telephone call for me. "Hold on, Fred," I said. "If that call is what I'm afraid it is, you may have yourself a match. If so, watch out!" The call was what I'd feared. The excuse was a valid one, and the girl was so nice about it that I couldn't get angry at her, but as I hung up I realized I was furious. I grabbed my racket, ran down to the court and began hitting balls harder than I ever had before. Amazingly, most of them went in. I didn't let up when the match began, nor did I relent my all-out attack until it was over. Even on crucial points I would go for winners and make them. I was playing with an uncharacteristic determination even when ahead; in fact I was playing *out of my mind*. Somehow the anger had taken me beyond my own preconceived limitations; it took me beyond caution. After the match Fred shook my hand without looking in the least dejected. He'd run into a hurricane on that day which he couldn't handle, but he'd had fun trying. In fact, I'd played so well that he seemed glad to have been there to witness it, or as if he deserved some credit for my reaching that level—which of course he did.

I don't want to promote the idea of playing angry as the key to winning. If there was a key that day it was that I played sincerely. I was angry that evening and instead of trying to pretend otherwise, I expressed it appropriately through my tennis. It felt good, and it worked.

THE MEANING OF WINNING

The riddle of the meaning of competition didn't come clear to me until later, when I began to discover something about the nature of the will to win. The key insight into the meaning of winning occurred one day in the course of discussion with my father, who, as mentioned earlier, had introduced me to competition and had considered himself an avid competitor in the worlds of both sport and business. Many times previously we had argued about competition, with my taking the side that it was unhealthy and only brought out the worst in people. But this particular conversation transcended argument.

I began by pointing to surfing as an example of a form of recreation which didn't involve one in competitiveness. Reflecting on this remark, Dad asked, "But don't surfers in fact compete against the waves they ride? Don't they avoid the strength of the wave and exploit its weakness?"

"Yes, but they're not competing against any person; they're not trying to beat anyone," I replied.

"No, but they are trying to make it to the beach, aren't they?"

"Yes, but the real point for the surfer is to get into the flow of the wave and perhaps to achieve oneness with it." But then it hit me. Dad was right; the surfer does want to ride the wave to the beach, yet he waits in the ocean for the biggest wave to come along that he thinks he can handle. If he just wanted to be "in the flow," he could do that on a medium-size wave. Why does the surfer wait for the big wave? The answer was simple, and it unraveled the confusion that surrounds the true nature of competition. The surfer waits for the big wave because he values the challenge it presents. He values the obstacles the wave puts between him and his goal of riding the wave to the beach. Why? Because it is those very obstacles, the size and churning power of the wave, which draw from the surfer his greatest effort. It is only against the big waves that he is required to use all his skill, all his courage and concentration to overcome; only then can he realize the true limits of his capacities. At that point he often attains his peak. In other words, the more challenging the obstacle he faces, the greater the opportunity for the surfer to discover and extend his true potential. The potential may have always been within him, but until it is manifested in action, it remains a secret hidden from himself. The obstacles are a very necessary ingredient to this process of self-discovery. Note that the surfer in this example is not out to *prove* himself; he is not out to show himself or the world how great he is, but is simply involved in the exploration of his latent capacities. He directly and intimately experiences his own resources and thereby increases his self-knowledge.

From this example the basic meaning of winning became more clear to me. *Winning is overcoming obstacles to reach a goal, but the value in winning is only as great as the value of the goal reached.* Reaching the goal itself may not be as valuable as the experience that can come in making a supreme effort to overcome the obstacles involved. The process can be more rewarding than the victory itself.

Once one recognizes the value of having difficult obstacles to overcome, it is a simple matter to see the true benefit that can be gained from competitive sports. In tennis who is it that provides a person with the obstacles he needs in order to experience his highest limits? His opponent, of course! Then is your opponent a friend or an enemy? He is a friend to the extent that he does his best to make things difficult for you. Only by playing the role of your enemy does he become your true friend. Only by competing with you does he in fact cooperate! No one wants to stand around on the court waiting for the big wave. In this use of competition it is the duty of your opponent to create the greatest possible difficulties for you, just as it is yours to try to create obstacles for him. Only by doing this do you give each other the opportunity to find out to what heights each can rise.

So I arrived at the startling conclusion that true competition is identical with true cooperation. Each player tries his hardest to defeat the other, but in this use of competition it isn't the other *person* we are defeating; it is simply a matter of overcoming the obstacles he presents. In true competition no person is defeated. Both players benefit by their efforts to overcome the obstacles presented by the other. Like two bulls butting their heads against one another, both grow stronger and each participates in the development of the other.

This attitude can make a lot of changes in the way you approach a tennis match. In the first place, instead of hoping your opponent is going to double-fault, you actually wish that he'll get his first serve in. This desire for the ball to land inside the line helps you to achieve a better mental state for returning it. You tend to react faster and move better, and by doing so, you make it more challenging for your opponent. You tend to build confidence in your opponent as well as in yourself and this greatly aids your sense of anticipation. Then at the end you shake hands with your opponent, and regardless of who won you thank him for the fight he put up, and you mean it.

I used to think that if I was playing a friendly match against a player with a weak backhand, it was a bit unfair to always play his weakness. In the light of the foregoing, nothing could be further from the truth! If you play his backhand as much as you can, it can only get better as a result. If you are a nice guy and play his forehand, his backhand will remain weak; in this case the real nice guy is the competitor.

This same insight into the nature of true competition led to yet another reversal in my thinking which greatly benefited my playing. Once when I was fifteen I upset an eighteen-year-old in a local tournament. After the match my father came down from the stands and heartily congratulated me for my victory, but my mother's reaction was, "Oh, that poor boy; how badly he must feel to have been beaten by someone so much younger." It was a clear example of the psyche pulled against itself. I felt pride and guilt simultaneously. Until I realized the purpose of competition, I never felt really happy about defeating someone, and mentally I had my hardest time playing well when I was near victory. I have found this to be true with many players, especially when on the verge of an upset. One cause of the uptightness experienced at these times is based on the false notion about competition. If I assume that I am making myself more worthy of respect by winning, then I must believe, consciously or unconsciously, that by defeating someone, I am making him less worthy of respect. I can't go up without pushing someone else down. This belief involves us in a needless sense of guilt. You don't have to become a killer to be a winner; you merely have to realize that killing is not the name of the game. Today I play every point to win. It's simple and it's good. I don't worry about winning or losing the match, but whether or not I am making the maximum effort during every point because I realize that that is where the true value lies.

Maximum effort does not mean the super-exertion of Self 1. It means concentration, determination and trusting your body to "let it happen." It means maximum physical and mental effort. Again competition and cooperation become one.

The difference between being concerned about winning and being concerned about making the effort to win may seem subtle, but in the effect there is a great difference. When I'm concerned only about winning, I'm caring about something that I can't wholly control. Whether I win or lose the external game is a result of my opponent's skill and effort as well as my own. When one is emotionally attached to results that he can't control, he tends to become anxious and then try too hard. But one can control the *effort* he puts into winning. One can always do the best he can at any given moment. Since it is impossible to feel anxiety about an event that one *can* control, the mere awareness that you are using maximum effort to win each point will carry you past the problem of anxiety. As a result, the energy which would otherwise have gone into the anxiety and its consequences can then be utilized in one's effort to win the point. In this way one's chances of winning the outer game are maximized.

Thus, for the player of the Inner Game, it is the moment-by-moment effort to let go and to stay centered in the here-and-now action which offers the real winning and losing, and this game never ends. One final word of caution. It is said that all great things are achieved by great effort. Although I believe that is true, it is not necessarily true that all great effort leads to greatness. A very wise person once told me, "When it comes to overcoming obstacles, there are three kinds of people. The first kind sees most obstacles as insurmountable and walks away. The second kind sees an obstacle and says, I can overcome it, and starts to dig under, climb over, or blast through it. The third type of person, before deciding to overcome the obstacle, tries to find a viewpoint where what is on the other side of the obstacle can be seen. Then, only if the reward is worth the effort, does he attempt to overcome the obstacle."

TEN

The Inner Game
Off the Court

UP TO THIS POINT WE HAVE BEEN EXPLORING THE INNER GAME AS IT applies to tennis. We began with the observation that many of our difficulties in tennis are mental in origin. As tennis players we tend to think too much before and during our shots; we try too hard to control our movements; and we are too concerned about the results of our actions and how they might reflect on our self-image. In short, we worry too much and don't concentrate very well. To gain clarity on the mental problems in tennis we introduced the concept of Self 1 and Self 2. Self 1 was the name given to the conscious ego-mind which likes to tell Self 2, you and your potential, how to hit the tennis ball. The key to spontaneous, high-level tennis is in resolving the lack of harmony which usually exists between these two selves. This requires the learning of several inner skills, chiefly the art of letting go of self-judgments, letting Self 2 do the hitting, recognizing and trusting the natural learning process, and above all gaining some practical experience in the art of relaxed concentration.

At this point the concept of the Inner Game emerges. Not only can these inner skills have a remarkable effect on one's forehand, backhand, serve and volley (the outer game of tennis), but they are valuable in themselves and have broad applicability to other aspects of life. When a player comes to recognize, for instance, that learning to focus may be more valuable to him than a backhand, he shifts from being primarily a player of the outer game to being a player of the Inner Game. Then, instead of learning focus to improve his tennis, he practices tennis to improve his focus. This represents a crucial shift in values from the outer to the inner. Only when this shift occurs within a player does he free himself of the anxieties and frustrations involved in being overly dependent on the results of the external game. Only then does he have the chance to go beyond the limitations inherent in the various ego trips of Self 1 and to reach a new awareness of his true potential. Competition then becomes an interesting device in which each player, by making his maximum effort to win, gives the other the opportunity he desires to reach new levels of self-awareness.

Thus, there are two games involved in tennis: one the outer game played against the obstacles presented by an external opponent and played for one or more external prizes; the other, the Inner Game, played against internal mental and emotional obstacles for the reward of knowledge and expression of one's true potential. It should be recognized that both the inner and outer games go on simultaneously, so the choice is not which one to play, but which deserves priority.

Clearly, almost every human activity involves both the outer and inner games. There are always external obstacles between us and our external goals, whether we are seeking wealth, education, reputation, friendship, peace on earth or simply something to eat for dinner. And the inner obstacles are always there; the very mind we use in obtaining our external goals is easily distracted by its tendency to worry, regret or generally muddle the situation, thereby causing needless difficulties from within. It is helpful to realize that whereas our external goals are many and various and require the learning of many skills to achieve them, the inner obstacles come from only one source and the skills needed to overcome them remain constant. Until subdued, Self 1 is capable of producing fears, doubts and delusions wherever you are and whatever you are doing. Focus in tennis is fundamentally no different from the focus needed to perform any task or even to enjoy a symphony; learning to let go of the habit of judging yourself on the basis of your backhand is no different from forgetting the habit of judging your child or boss; and learning to welcome obstacles in competition automatically increases one's ability to find advantage in all the difficulties one meets in the course of one's life. Hence, every inner gain applies immediately and automatically to the full range of one's activities. This is why it is worthwhile to pay some attention to the inner game.

BUILDING INNER STABILITY

Perhaps the most indispensable tool for human beings in modern times is the ability to remain calm in the midst of rapid and unsettling changes. The people who will best survive the present age are the ones Kipling described as "those who can keep their heads while all about are losing theirs." Inner stability is achieved not by burying one's head in the sand at the sight of danger, but by acquiring the ability to see the true nature of what is happening and to respond appropriately. Then Self 1's reaction to the situation is not able to disrupt your inner balance or clarity.

Instability, in contrast, is a condition of being in which we are more easily thrown off balance when Self 1 gets upset by an event or circumstance. Self 1 tends to distort its perception of the event, prompting us to take misguided actions, which in turn leads to circumstances that further undermine our inner balance—the basic Self 1 vicious cycle.

People ask, "So how can I manage my stress?" Courses are taken, remedies offered, yet often the Self 1 stress continues. The problem with "managing stress" is that you tend to believe it is inevitable. There has to be the stress for you to manage. I've noticed that Self 1 tends to thrive when it is fought. An alternative approach is simply to build on your stability. Support and encourage your Self 2, knowing that the stronger it gets, the more it will take to throw you off balance, and the quicker you can regain your balance.

Self 1 stress is a thief that, if we let it, can rob us of the enjoyment of our lives. The longer I live, the greater my appreciation of the gift that life itself is. This gift is much greater than I could have imagined, and therefore time spent living it in a state of stress means I am missing a lot—on or off the court. Maybe wisdom is not so much to come up with new answers as to recognize at a deeper level the profundity of the age-old answers. Some things don't change. The need to trust oneself and grow in understanding of our true selves will never diminish. The need to let go of the lenses of "good–bad" judgment of ourselves and others will always be the doorway to the possibility of clarity. And the importance of being clear about one's priorities, especially the first priority in your life, will never become less important while you still have life.

Stress is easier than ever to come by in a time when pressures come toward us from all corners. Wives, husbands, bosses, children, bills, advertising, society itself, will continue to make their demands on our lives. "Do this better, do this more, be this way and don't be that way, make something of yourself, be more like him or be like her, we are now instituting these changes, so change." The message is no different from "Hit the ball this way or hit the ball that way, and you're no good if you don't." Sometimes the demands are put so sweetly or matter-of-factly that they seem an innocent part of life; sometimes they come so harshly that they provoke action out of fear. But one thing is for sure: the pressures from outside will keep on coming and in fact could easily accelerate in pace and increase in intensity. Information is exploding, and with it the need to know more and stretch our competencies. While the demands of work are increasing for most people, so is the threat of losing one's work.

The cause of most stress can be summed up by the word *attachment*. Self 1 gets so dependent upon things, situations, people and concepts within its experience that when change occurs or seems about to occur, it feels threatened. Freedom from stress does not necessarily involve giving up anything, but rather being able to let go of anything, when necessary, and know that one will still be all right. It comes from being more independent—not necessarily more solitary, but more reliant on one's own inner resources for stability.

The wisdom of building inner stability in such times seems to me to be an obvious requirement for successful living. The first step toward inner stability may be the acknowledgment that there is an inner self that has inherent needs of its own. The self that has all your gifts and capabilities, with which you hope to accomplish anything, has its own requirements. They are natural demands that we didn't even have to be taught. Each Self 2 is endowed by birth, regardless of where that birth took place, with an instinct to fulfill its nature. It wants to enjoy, to learn, to understand, appreciate, go for it, rest, be healthy, survive, be free to be what it is, express itself and make its unique contribution.

Self 2's needs come with a gentle but constant urging. A certain feeling of contentment attends a person whenever he or she is acting in sync with this self. The fundamental issue is what kind of priority are we giving the demands of Self 2 in relation to all the external pressures? It is obvious that every individual must ask and answer this question for himself or herself.

I, like anyone else, have to learn something very important—how to distinguish the inner requests of Self 2 from the outer demands that have been "internalized" by Self 1 and are now so familiar in my thinking that they "sound like" they are coming from me. Being self-employed for twenty-five years, I admit that

I have been my own worst stressor. But slowly I have found that the demands I'm trying to fulfill when I'm stressing myself are not really my own, but ones I have "picked up" or "bought into" for perhaps no better reason than I heard them early in life, or because they seemed to be so generally accepted. Soon they begin to sound right—and are therefore easier to listen to than the subtle but insistent urging of my own being.

One of my favorite interviews with a tennis player was one that took place with Jennifer Capriati when she was fourteen years old. At the time, she was playing in world-class women's tournaments and doing remarkably well. The reporter was asking her how nervous she got when she was playing against some of the best players in the world. Jennifer responded that she didn't get nervous at all. She said she considered it a privilege to play with these players, something she hadn't been able to do up until that time. "But surely when you are in the semifinals of a world-class tournament, and being only fourteen, with all the expectations that are on you, you must experience some stress." Jennifer's final answer to all the reporter's probing for her fear was simple, innocent and, as far as I can see, pure Self 2. "If I was feeling frightened playing tennis, I don't see why I would do it!" she exclaimed. With that the reporter stopped her questioning.

Perhaps the cynic in us wants to say, "But look at what happened to Jennifer later." Yes, she may have lost a few rounds to Self 1, but the match isn't over in a single victory or a single defeat. Self 1 doesn't give up easily, nor does Self 2. That Jennifer's Self 2 is fully intact, I have no doubt. We could well take inspiration from her example at fourteen of putting fear in its place.

Freedom from stress happens in proportion to our responsiveness to our true selves, allowing every moment possible to be an opportunity for Self 2 to be what it is and enjoy the process. As far as I can see, this is a lifelong learning process.

I hope by now you have understood that I am not promoting the kind of positive thinking that tries to assert mentally that things are wonderful when they aren't. And not the kind that says,

"If I think I'm kind, then I am; if I think I'm a winner, then I am." As far as I'm concerned, this is Self 1 trying to make a better Self 1. The dog chases its own tail.

In most lectures that I have given recently, I remind myself and the audience that even though I come from California, I don't believe in self-improvement, and I certainly don't want to improve them. Sometimes there is a stunned response. But I don't think anyone's Self 2 needs improvement from birth to death. It has always been fine. I, more than anyone, need to remember that. Yes, our backhands can improve, and I'm sure my writing can get better; certainly our skills in relating to each other on the planet can improve. But the cornerstone of stability is to know that there is nothing wrong with the essential human being.

Believe me, I do not say this without due regard to the depths of disruption that can be caused by Self 1, but out of a knowledge born from personal experience that there is always a part of us that remains immune to the contamination of Self 1. Perhaps I have to learn and relearn this fact because I was conditioned so early to believe the opposite: that somehow I was bad and had to learn to become good.

The part of my life spent trying to compensate for this negativity by being extra good has been neither enjoyable nor rewarding. Although I usually managed to live up to and sometimes surpass the expectations of those I was trying to please or appease, it was not without a cost to my connection with myself. My explorations of the Inner Game of Tennis helped me to see in a very practical way that Self 2, left to its own resources, did very well on its own. I expect I'll never outgrow the need to renew trust in myself and to protect myself from the voices, inside or out, that undermine that trust.

What else can be done to promote stability? The message of the Inner Game is simple: focus. Focus of attention in the present moment, the only one you can really live in, is at the heart of this book and at the heart of the art of doing anything well. Focus means not dwelling on the past, either on mistakes or glories; it means not being so caught up in the future, either its fears or its dreams, that my full attention is taken from the present. The ability to focus the mind is the ability to not let it run away with you. It does not mean not to think—but to be the one who directs your own thinking. Focusing can be practiced on a tennis court, chopping carrots, in a pressure-packed board meeting or while driving in traffic. It can be practiced when alone or in conversation. It takes as much trust to fully focus attention when listening to another person without carrying on a side conversation in your own head as it does to watch a tennis ball in all its detail, without listening to Self 1's worries, hopes and instructions.

Stability grows as I learn to accept what I cannot control and take control of what I can. One cold winter evening, on my first year after graduation from college, I learned for the first but by no means the last time about the power of acceptance of life and death. I was alone, driving my Volkswagen bug to Exeter, New Hampshire, from a small town in Maine. It was near midnight when my wheel skidded on an icy curve and spun my car gently but firmly off the road and into a snowbank.

As I sat in the car getting colder by the second, the gravity of my situation struck me. It was about twenty degrees below zero outside, and I had nothing other than the sport jacket I was wearing. There was no hope of keeping warm in the car while it was stationary, and there was little hope of being picked up by another car. It had been twenty minutes since I had passed through a town, and not a single automobile had passed me in that time. There were no farmhouses, no cultivated land, not even telephone poles to remind me of civilization. I had no map and no idea how far ahead the next town might be.

I was faced with an interesting choice. I would freeze if I remained in the car, so I had to decide whether to walk forward into the unknown in the hope that a town might be around the very next corner, or to walk back in the direction from which I had come, knowing that there was certain help at least fifteen miles back. After deliberating for a moment, I decided to take my chances with the unknown. After all, isn't that what they do in the movies? I walked forward for about ten steps and then, without thinking, pivoted decisively and walked back the other way.

After three minutes, my ears were freezing and felt as if they were about to chip off, so I started to run. But the cold drained my energy quickly, and soon I had to slow again to a walk. This time I walked for only two minutes before becoming too cold. Again I ran, but again grew fatigued quickly. The periods of running began to grow shorter, as did the periods of walking, and I soon realized what the outcome of these decreasing cycles would be. I could see myself by the side of the road covered with snow and frozen stiff. At that moment, what had first appeared to be merely a difficult situation began to look as if it was going to be my final situation. Awareness of the very possibility of death slowed me to a stop.

After a minute of reflection, I found myself saying aloud, "Okay, if now is the time, so be it. I'm ready." I really meant it. With that I stopped thinking about it and began walking calmly down the road, suddenly aware of the beauty of the night. I became absorbed in the silence of the stars and in the loveliness of the dimly lit forms around me; everything was beautiful. Then without thinking, I started running. To my surprise I didn't stop for a full forty minutes, and then only because I spotted a light burning in the window of a distant house.

Where had this energy come from that allowed me to run so far without stopping? I hadn't felt frightened; I simply didn't get tired or cold. As I relate this story now, it seems that saying "I accepted death" is ambiguous. I didn't give up in the sense of quitting. In one sense I gave up one kind of caring and was imbued with another. Apparently, letting go of my grip on life released an energy that paradoxically made it possible for me to run with utter abandon *toward* life.

"Abandon" is a good word to describe what happens to a tennis player who feels he has nothing to lose. He stops caring about the outcome and plays all out. It is a letting go of the concerns of

Self 1 and letting in of the natural concerns of a deeper and truer self. It is caring, yet not caring; it is effort, but effortless at the same time.

THE GOAL OF THE INNER GAME

Now we come to an interesting point, and the last one. We have talked about gaining more access to Self 2 and about getting out of our own way so that we could perform and learn better in whatever outer games we choose to play. Focus, trust, choice, nonjudgmental awareness were all recommended as tools for this end. But one question has not been raised. What does it mean to *win* the Inner Game?

A few years ago, I might have tried to answer this question. Now I choose not to—even though I think it is the most important question. Any attempt to define an answer to this question is an invitation to Self 1 to form a misconception. Self 1, in fact, has come a long way if it has gotten to the point where it can admit, and mean it, that it doesn't know and never will. Then the individual has more of a chance to feel the need of his own being, to follow the inner thirst and to discover what is truly satisfying. That my Self 2 will be the only one who knows—that there will be no external credit or praise—is something I greet with relief.

LOOKING FORWARD

Sometimes I am asked about my vision for the future of the inner game. This game has been going on well before I was born and will go on well after I die. It is not for me to have a vision for it; it has its own vision. I feel fortunate enough to have the chance to witness and enjoy it.

Regarding the Inner Game with capital letters, i.e., the development and applications of the methods and principles articulated in the Inner Game books, I believe they will become more and more important during the next century. I honestly believe that during the past few hundred years, mankind has been so absorbed with overcoming external challenges that the essential need to focus on inner challenges has been neglected.

In sports, I would like to see teaching professionals of all sports become equally competent in both domains—able to guide the development of both the external and the inner skills of their students. As they do so, a greater dignity will come to their profession as well as to those who play sports.

I believe the areas of business, health, education and human relationships will evolve in the understanding of human development and the inner skills they require. We will become better learners and more independent thinkers. In short, I believe we are still just at the beginning of a profound and long-needed rebalancing process between outer and inner. This is not me-ism. It is a process of self-discovery that naturally makes its own contribution to the whole as we learn to make the basic contribution to ourselves.